brilliant project management

WITHDRAWN

brilliant project management

management

What the best project managers
know, say and do

Stephen Barker and
Rob Cole

PEARSON
Prentice Hall
BUSINESS

Harlow, England • London • New York • Boston • San Francisco • Toronto
Sydney • Tokyo • Singapore • Hong Kong • Seoul • Taipei • New Delhi
Cape Town • Madrid • Mexico City • Amsterdam • Munich • Paris • Milan

PEARSON EDUCATION LIMITED

Edinburgh Gate
Harlow CM20 2JE
Tel: +44 (0) 1279 623623
Fax: +44 (0) 1279 431059
Website: www.pearsoned.co.uk

First published in Great Britain in 2007

ISBN 978 0 273 70793 6

British Library Cataloguing-in-Publication Data
A catalogue record for this book is available from the British Library

Library of Congress Cataloging-in-Publication Data
Cole, Rob.
  Brilliant project management : what the best project managers know, say and do / Rob Cole and Stephen Barker.
    p. cm.
  Includes index.
  ISBN 978-0-273-70793-6
  1. Project management. I. Barker, Stephen, 1964- II. Title.

HD69.P75C635 2007
658.4'04–dc22

2006053270

10 9 8 7 6 5 4 3
11 10 09 08 07

Cartoons by Ken Pyne
Typeset in 10/14 pt in Latin725 BT by 3
Printed by Ashford Colour Press Ltd., Gosport

The publisher's policy is to use paper manufactured from sustainable forests.

Dedications

For Alfie & Cissie, Ella Grace

Ellie and Will

Contents

Acknowledgements

In some ways finalising these acknowledgements has been the hardest part of writing this book. So many people have contributed both directly and indirectly – and sometimes unknowingly. It would be impossible to name everyone here, but we're sure you'll let us know that we owe you a drink – maybe even a couple!

We'd like to start by thanking all the people we've worked with over recent years. They've not only helped us to deliver projects, they've sparked many of our ideas. We'd also like to record our appreciation for everyone who reviewed our draft material. Their feedback was very useful and gave us plenty of encouragement. We're grateful to the team at Pearson too, for making the book happen. Everyone there made us feel this project was very important.

All kinds of other people have had a positive effect on us and have influenced this book in subtler ways: family, friends and fellow professionals. Over the years, they've helped us to keep a sense of perspective and *tried* to stop us from taking ourselves too seriously. And none of this would have happened without the support of Rachel Stock, who saw potential in our rough early work and persuaded her colleagues at Pearson to commission the book.

Last of all, we want to save the biggest thank you for Caroline and Louise for their unwavering tolerance and good humour. Without any hint of complaint, they supported us through the many hours we were locked away writing and holding endless conference calls. We've got a feeling we're now in debt for more than a few light refreshments!

How to contact the authors:

- Stephen Barker – stephen.barker@barkerandcole.co.uk
- Rob Cole – rob.cole@barkerandcole.co.uk

Chapter one

the
road
to brilliant
project
management

a street guide

> **"**The worth of a book is to be measured by what you can carry away from it. **"**

James Bryce (1838–1922)

Introduction

Do you have a burning desire to be a brilliant project manager? Are you relatively new to project management and keen to develop your skills quickly? Or are you an experienced professional looking for a refresher? If your head is nodding then you're just the kind of person this practical guide is for.

In this book we've distilled down what we think it takes to be a brilliant project manager. We've drawn on the good, the bad and the ugly – and the eccentric. But above all, we've thought long and hard about what we've learned from rolling up our sleeves and getting our hands dirty. Between us we've got over 30 years of hands-on project management experience. That's plenty of time to learn lessons at the school of hard knocks!

Barker & Cole's home truths

Experience alone is unlikely to make you a brilliant project manager. You'll also need to do your own research and get good advice along the way.

The buck stops here

You've probably noticed that projects don't always run according to plan. In fact, you may have concluded that spiralling budgets, missed deadlines and half-baked deliveries are the norm rather than the exception. It's certainly true that failures are commonplace and some surveys put the rate as high as 70%. So what keeps going wrong?

Much of this is down to projects being inadequately planned and poorly managed. Responsibility for this has to be placed at the project manager's door. This might seem a harsh assessment when external factors contribute to failure, but project managers are ultimately held accountable for the fate of their projects. Failures can't solely be put down to inexperience either, since even hardened project managers are seen leading their projects down paths that can only end in disaster.

There are project managers – we've dubbed them *brilliant project managers* – who consistently succeed. This select group has the winning knack of regularly delivering the goods and we're going to share the techniques they use. The good news is: none of it is complicated advice. What we have to offer is based on a combination of good old-fashioned common sense, practical experience of what works well and knowledge of the pitfalls to avoid.

What's in this book?

Project management can seem a solitary trade at times but *you're not alone*. Many of the day-to-day issues you'll come across have already been tackled before and *Brilliant Project Management* passes on this experience.

Barker & Cole's top tips

Next time you're preparing for a meeting to discuss a new project, take an hour out beforehand to dip into *Brilliant Project Management*.

Our advice has been packaged as a *guide book* to project management. You can dip into the topics that interest you most or read it from cover to cover. Like any guide book, we've had to be selective about the subjects we explore. However, we've focused our attention on what you'll find of most practical use and can immediately apply. We'll show you the tricks of the trade and the traps to avoid. Best of all, this advice is tried and tested in the real world of project management.

We've got plenty to say about the traditional project management topics, as well as the people side of the job that often gets overlooked. Project managers don't just struggle with the intricacies of plans and risk logs, they struggle with people too!

The topics we cover in this book

Core project management skills

Planning projects, dealing with risks and issues, delivering quality, resource planning and management

People-related skills

Providing leadership, running effective meetings, facilitation techniques

▶

> **Learning lessons**
>
> Benefiting from experience

We recognise that becoming a brilliant project manager takes much more than reading a book; there's no substitute for practical experience. But as you develop your skills, we hope you'll turn to this book for a reminder of the good practice it's so easy to forget during the daily cut and thrust. We say this based on our experience of writing this book, gaining so much from another look at familiar ground during the process. In fact, our catchphrase soon became: 'Wow! This is good advice; we should be doing this ourselves!' *Most of the time*, we were only joking.

Five reasons why it's great to be a project manager

1 *Work is interesting and challenging.* You'll be kept busy solving one problem or another, and there's never a dull moment!

2 *There's plenty of job satisfaction.* Especially when you see something through to completion.

3 *Variety is the spice of life.* No two projects are exactly the same and there's always something new to learn.

4 *It's a people business.* You get to work with all sorts of interesting types.

5 *You'll never be short of work.* The world will never run out of projects that need managing.

Before you set off

The journey to brilliant project management is an absorbing one, with plenty to see and do along the way. But you don't need to travel alone. We hope you'll find us useful tour guides for at least part of the way.

Barker & Cole's final word on *starting off* ...

A skilled specialist accepted a job as a project manager. Years of watching others in action – both good and bad – provided her with plenty of ideas about how to do a brilliant job. Mentored by an experienced colleague, she took to the role with enthusiasm. The project was fraught with problems, went over budget and was delivered very late – but it was like being on an intense training programme. Within 18 months she was trouble-shooting problematic projects and mentoring junior managers.

Managing demanding projects is a great way to learn quickly. It may seem hard at the time but there's no substitute for on-the-job training in challenging circumstances.

the art
of planning a project

sharpening the axe

> **"**A good plan today is better than a perfect plan tomorrow.**"**

George S. Patton (1885–1945)

Introduction

Too many projects start life doomed to failure. Poorly defined business requirements and unrealistic delivery deadlines are all too common. Projects start unravelling from day one with the project manager acting like an innocent bystander to an accident that was waiting to happen. There are many reasons why projects fail, but more often than not an important root cause is in the initial planning process – or rather lack of one.

A brilliant project manager knows that putting together a credible and robust plan is one of the foundation stones of effective project management. Although planning is as much an art as it is an exact science, prior experience and common sense both have a big part to play. There are also some sound guiding principles that anyone can pick up and run with.

Your planning skills will be called upon from the moment you take over a project. The chances are you'll inherit either an unrealistic plan or nothing concrete at all. Don't be surprised if deadlines and under-pinning assumptions delivered in the initial project package are peppered with unfounded optimism.

Not all is lost, though, and paradoxically the worse the starting point is, the greater the opportunity for turning things around. Brilliant project managers have to be able to rescue projects in dire straits and in fact they delight in achieving this. The road to recovery starts with building a credible project plan.

Does my project have a chequered past?

You're in trouble when…

- The project has changed its name at least once to try to leave its past behind and to restore its good reputation.

- You're the latest in a long succession of project managers.

- Other project managers seem far too pleased that this particular project has fallen to you.

- Your project has already been running for a very long time without delivering anything.

Before we look at what makes a good plan and how to go about producing one, let's start at the point at which things begin to get interesting: the point at which a project is handed to a project manager.

Taking on a project

For a brilliant project manager, the definition of the start of the project is simply when responsibility is handed over. Most projects will already be up and running in some shape or form when you take over, and in the worst case scenario your new project will already have a chequered past. Even if you join a project relatively early on, it's likely some work will be under way or completed. Perhaps somebody's already recruited a couple of team members ahead of your arrival and they're cracking on with what they see as the immediate priorities.

At the start of a new assignment you'll need all your wits about you. Taking on responsibility for a new project is a defining moment for a project manager. There's always a short honeymoon period when it's reasonable to question – in a constructive way – what's gone on before and to recommend corrective action. It's vital to use this initial handover period to best advantage and to carry out a rapid health check. When you uncover shortcomings, you'll also need the skills to get your project back on track as quickly as possible.

A quick project health check: five good starting questions

1   Are the project's objectives clear and measurable?

2   Has anyone documented what the project needs to deliver – and have your customers signed up to this?

3   At first sight, do existing commitments to deliverables, timescales and resources look realistic?

4   If work is already well under way, is there a clear audit trail of significant decisions taken and underpinning assumptions?

5   Is your team working together productively and does everyone know what they're expected to deliver?

Although it's impossible to legislate for all handover scenarios, there's a reliable technique for embarking upon a new project with eyes at least partially open, rather than tightly shut. This starts with making sure there's a robust and appropriate project plan in place – and if not, developing one as soon as possible.

Barker & Cole's home truths

Taking over a project that's 'pretty much finished – with just a few loose ends to tidy up' can be the ultimate doomsday scenario. Others can be prone to wishful thinking when assessing what it takes to complete a project.

What makes a good plan?

The plan captures in one concise document what you've been asked to do and how you intend to deliver. It documents all the key points relating to a project ranging from its objectives and deliverables right through to the key milestones and resource requirements. A good plan is one of the foundation stones for any project and should inspire confidence in all concerned.

The mere act of creating a plan is an excellent health check in itself. Producing one is the quickest way for you to diagnose problems and begin addressing them. In a well-defined and properly set-up project this should be a simple process. For projects built on a foundation of sand – and there are plenty of them – this will prove to be a challenging task.

An imperfect plan is better than none at all. It's useful to publish a warts-and-all document as an opening gambit even if it has obvious flaws. Your audience can then help you to refine it. This is usually a more productive approach than spending an inordinate amount of time trying to produce something close to perfection first time round.

A plan is much more than a schedule

The difference between a project plan and a project schedule confuses many project managers. If you ask a random cross section of them to show you their project *plan*, most will whip out their *schedule* – usually in the form of a popular type of bar chart known as a Gantt chart. There's a big difference between these two key documents and what they're used for.

A schedule usually lays out project tasks and timings, and perhaps lists important milestones. The schedule enables a project manager to monitor and control progress as work proceeds. A brilliant project plan contains the project schedule, but a lot more besides.

The table opposite shows you what you should expect to find in a plan.

Section	Typical contents
Overview	A summary of the project's key features including its objectives and how to meet them.
Objectives and key requirements	A clear description of the project's objectives spelling out what the project needs to achieve to fulfil its business case. Plus a list of the corresponding key requirements that must be met.
Approach	A description of how the project is going to be tackled, including the stages it will be broken into and any standards to be adhered to.
Major deliverables and key milestones	A summary of the project's outputs and their delivery timescales.
Scope	A clear description of the boundary that will be drawn around the scope of the project, identifying the key items that are both inside and outside the scope.
Resource needs	A summary of all of the resources that are required to complete the project, broken down by type of resource.
Organisation/roles and responsibilities	A list of the major project roles, the extent of their responsibilities and how the people resources will be organised.
Internal and external dependencies	A list of the project's important dependencies. Some will be within its control, while others will involve third parties.
Assumptions	A list of the assumptions that have been used in preparing the project plan.
Implementation strategy	A description of how the project deliverables will be put into service.
Schedule	A diagrammatic view of major project phases, milestones, activities, tasks and the resources allocated to each task.
Risk and issue management	An initial log of the project's key risks and issues, together with how they'll be managed.
Quality assurance and control strategy	A description of the processes that will be used to make sure the project's deliverables are fit for purpose.
Configuration management	The procedures that will be used to manage the versions of the various project deliverables.

Planning essentials

Within the contents of the comprehensive plan we've suggested, there are specific areas that deserve particular attention. These topics represent the foundations of your plan and correspond to the five *minimum* areas that any plan should address.

Five critical elements of any good plan

1   Project objectives and supporting key requirements.

2   Project scope.

3   Major deliverables.

4   Resource needs.

5   The project schedule with key delivery dates.

The rest of this chapter is devoted to looking at each of these five areas in turn. Although as a project manager you're most likely to be quizzed first about delivery dates!

1 Clarifying project objectives

In planning a project, it's essential that the customers have a good understanding of its underlying objectives and the most important requirements. If your customers are not clear about what they want to achieve, your job of putting together a plan is made more difficult. It also raises serious questions about the wisdom of proceeding any further.

This might seem an obvious point but it never ceases to amaze us how many projects fail this simple test. At the beginning of a project, you'll often be faced with hazy objectives and requirements. If that's the case, getting these fundamentals clarified must become an important early aim of your project, before it goes any further off track.

We're not suggesting that objectives and requirements need to be defined in fine detail from the outset. However we do believe that, before work starts in earnest, it's important for you and your customers to achieve a shared understanding of the 'Big Picture'. So on a construction project, for example, it's a distinct advantage to know whether you're building a bungalow or hotel before starting work on the foundations!

It's important to distinguish between a project *objective* and a project *requirement*. Objectives describe the desired outcome for the project as a whole; for example, 'to build a house that will be attractive to, and affordable for, first-time buyers'. Requirements, on the other hand, specify what needs to be delivered; for example, 'the house must have two doubles and one single bedroom'.

It shouldn't happen to a project manager (but it did) . . .

A project manager was assigned to an IT project that had been running for several years. Considerable effort had been devoted to drawing up a complex statement of requirements. The project's major deliverable – for some considerable outlay – was to be the *NEF* system. Eager to find out more about what lay behind the system, she located the section on objectives in the weighty requirements documentation. It contained one sentence: 'The objective of the *NEF* project is to deliver the *NEF* system.'

Running a project without a clear understanding of the underlying business objectives is like playing a game of chess without being introduced to the term 'check-mate'. You're going to have trouble finishing the game.

It's not unusual to find that customers have developed a detailed view of what they *want* without giving a great deal of thought to what they'd like the project to *achieve*. You may even find that some customers see any discussion of the project objectives as stretching beyond your remit: 'Leave the whys and wherefores to me, and just concentrate on delivering what I want.'

It's in your own best interests to avoid being swayed by this view. If the project objectives are nailed down, it's easier to help your customers check that the key requirements cross-match and support the objectives. In the final analysis, the project will be measured against the customer's expectations. It's much easier for customers to say, 'This isn't what I asked for,' when they have not been pressed to clarify what they wanted in the first place.

Finally, if your customers can't spell out their rationale for the project, it can still proceed – in these circumstances many do and some succeed. However, pinning them down will dramatically increase the odds of a positive outcome.

2 Pinning down the scope

All projects need a sound statement of scope. This describes the boundary to be drawn around what the project will and will not deliver. Quite often project sponsors actively want to avoid defining scope *too tightly* – they feel it will stifle their creativity and limit their ability to flesh out requirements. However, there's a balance that must be struck here and it's important to avoid being too woolly.

Having a clear definition of scope doesn't lock anyone into a particular path come-what-may, but it *does* provide a sound baseline to manage change against. This allows a project manager to make sure everyone understands the impact of scope adjustments and should not be confused with trying to prevent change. This way, the project team is able to identify any extra work required and to agree any additional costs. A clear definition is mutually beneficial.

On any project there is a risk of 'scope creep' – the gradual process of the work expanding without the implications being managed effectively. Everyone has personal experience of this phenomenon: ranging from the wildly expensive home improvement project that started life as a quick makeover, to the bank-balance-busting shopping trip that began life as a quest for a single item of work clothing.

Barker & Cole's top tips

Spell out what's *not* going to be addressed by the project as well as specifying what *is* within scope. Don't rely on everyone making the same assumptions about what is 'obviously' implied.

You should also clearly state what's not included in the asking price from day one, rather than finding a difference in expectations after the event, with all the recriminations that will inevitably follow. For example, if your house-building project isn't going to fit out the kitchen, clearly say so from the outset. It's in everyone's best interests to avoid fundamental misunderstandings from the very start.

3 Defining major deliverables

No sane person would entertain the idea of engaging a construction company with the simple remit to '*build a house*'. At the very least there would have to be a statement of the expected deliverables such as: a three-bedroom house with two bathrooms and a landscaped garden, plus supporting items like architect's drawings and a garden design.

This basic principle should be applied to every project – make sure all the tangible things are defined and agreed up front. It shouldn't be

ɔu to define your project this way. If this *is* a difficult task,
,et a timely warning regarding your lack of understanding
what needs to be delivered.

> ### Barker & Cole's top tips
>
> Do a sanity check of your major deliverables against your objectives to check they're aligned. Every one should relate directly or indirectly to the project objectives – and vice versa.

The benefits of focusing on deliverables rather than activities can be seen from the very start. A project based on tangible deliverables is far easier to manage. It allows you to be precise about what needs to be delivered and helps you to track progress in a concrete way.

4 Realistic resources

Your project sponsor will want to keep a close eye on costs and one of the key questions will be: *how much*? You'll be under immediate pressure to keep a lid on resources and costs, or perhaps even achieve a reduction. There's certainly nothing wrong with fiscal prudence but this pressure will occasionally border on the farcical. Be wary of demands to reduce costs when the budget is already optimistic or perform other similar acts of financial wizardry.

It's important to resist early pressure to adopt an unrealistic budget. While it's unlikely you'll be asked to slash the budget without reason and the argument put forward may be persuasive, be wary of accepting it at face value. For example, the customer may insist, 'We don't want a gold-plated solution.' In reality, this type of discussion is rarely about overly elaborate requirements, it's more about miraculously achieving reduced costs without any consequences. Roughly translated into real project-speak this means: 'We want everything we've asked for but at a discounted cost.'

Having got an agreed budget, the first priority for a project manager is to identify and manage those costs that'll be assigned to your project; primarily anything you'll need to buy or hire to build the project's deliverables. This may include the cost of equipment purchased or funds needed to cover the expense of hiring external project team members. Since these costs are a direct result of your project, you'll be expected to prepare an accurate budget for them and then to be held accountable for the expenditure.

You can afford to take a more relaxed view of any general overheads that are not directly connected with your project; for example bills for heating and lighting. We're not advocating that a project manager should intentionally ignore known costs but effort spent chasing wider costs is effort lost to other project management tasks. You'll rarely be expected to factor in these costs and doing so only opens up a can of financial worms. Leave well alone!

Key costs to consider when you're preparing your budget

1   People costs charged to your project including external contractors and consultants.

2   Equipment purchased or hired to deliver the project. For example machinery or supporting technology.

3   Facilities your project needs and has direct responsibility for. For example rented temporary accommodation.

4   Expenses incurred when the fruits of your labours are first handed over. For example training, marketing and one-off deployment costs.

5   Costs your customers will incur to keep what you have delivered operating from day to day.

We know it's not easy to deal with a situation where a realistic budget is out of kilter with expectations. In order to defend what might be seen as an unreasonable proposal, you'll need to have a clear audit trail of how cost estimates have been arrived at. This should include a detailed breakdown of how you arrived at the overall cost and highlight any key assumptions used.

Identifying resource costs for the project plan is just the start of the process. Careful resource planning and management is an important part of brilliant project management. That's why we've dedicated the whole of Chapter 5 to this topic.

5 An achievable schedule

After the handover preliminaries are complete, the first question you'll be asked is, 'When can we see your project plan?' or the *project schedule,* as we now know it. Primarily your customers will want to know when you expect the project to deliver, but they'll also want some proof your dates were not just plucked out of thin air.

It's important to resist the temptation to come up with a crowd-pleasing initial offering with wildly optimistic delivery dates. After the warm glow from the backslapping and congratulations fades you'll be left with a millstone round your neck for the remainder of the project. It's far better to set out your stall with a schedule that's realistic and well thought out.

You need to understand your customers' timing expectations, but the schedule shouldn't be built around these exclusively. Too many planning exercises are doomed from the beginning because they start from an imposed delivery date and work backwards. In contrast, a brilliant plan is based upon three key elements:

- *Deliverables* – what your project needs to deliver.
- *Resources* – the resources required to deliver your project.
- *Dependencies* – those dependencies between your items of work.

You should develop the schedule around a clear, logical structure for delivering the project. The first step is to break up the project into manageable chunks of work. For example in a construction project:

- put down the foundations;
- lay the brickwork;
- add the roofing;

- fit the windows, and
- finish off the interior.

This structure will usually be based on the major deliverables and it must reflect the sequence of delivery or any interdependencies.

It's important that you get the level of detail in the schedule right. The current phase should be sufficiently detailed to enable work to be tracked and reported on at least weekly. However, it will usually be sufficient to have activities for later project phases defined at a higher level of detail. Sufficient planning is required to provide reasonable confidence in the schedule, but a lot of work trying to define distant project activities is unlikely to be the best use of your time.

Top tips for developing a realistic schedule

1 *Develop a schedule for the complete project.* It should include a summary of all of the activities through to the project end. This may not be easy since early project phases may have a significant impact on the rest of the project. However, the schedule without an end is likely to be an accurate prediction: the project will never end.

2 *Provide clear visibility of the project's key deliverables.* Your schedule should show how and when the project's key deliverables are to be produced. The delivery of each key product should be flagged as a significant project milestone.

3 *Design the schedule to make tracking and reporting easy.* As the schedule is being developed, make sure it's structured to facilitate progress reporting too. Then you can publish a copy with progress reflected in it or extract the information for inclusion in a report.

Although you're the custodian of the project schedule, it's important to involve your team in its development. This is an excellent way to build commitment to the deadlines. Your project will be at serious risk of derailment if your team believes it's been put together without team members' input. When the going gets tough – which it will – your team might well spend more time finding fault with the schedule than getting on with the job.

Lastly, before final publication, commission a peer review from outside the team. There's much to be gained from asking a friendly colleague to run over the schedule with a 'fresh pair of eyes'. Select someone with the right experience who hasn't been involved in the planning process itself to provide an assessment of the schedule's overall completeness, clarity and feasibility.

It shouldn't happen to a project manager (but it did) ...

A project manager joined a project in dire straits – there was no chance of delivering to the agreed milestones. The company's finance director and programme manager demanded a new, realistic project plan (*schedule*) immediately. The project manager built a new schedule based on realistic timescales, using estimates provided by the delivery team. Milestones were tight but achievable.

The project team presented its plan and was shocked by the programme manager's response: 'Don't ever insult me like this again! I'm going to leave the room for an hour to calm down; I can't trust myself at the moment. When I return make sure your revised dates don't have the same effect.'

It's no fun feeling the heat when your schedule is unpopular. But you'll suffer a worse fate if you get bullied into committing to a schedule that's simply unachievable.

Summary

There's an enormous temptation at the start of a project to roll up your sleeves and get cracking – perhaps to start work on a highly visible, meaty project task and make an immediate impression as a doer. This is just like a builder starting to lay bricks before the architect is consulted. In contrast, when George Washington famously decided to fell a tree, he spent plenty of time sharpening the axe before a quick burst of activity completed his mission. We're strong advocates of this measured and *planned* approach.

Time set aside for producing a plan is likely to be the best investment you can make on inheriting a project. For a start, never, ever accept your new project is in good shape unless you can see it with your own eyes and prove it with hard facts. Make sure you begin by giving your project an immediate health check by taking a close look at the plan – assuming there is one – and double-checking it's built on solid foundations.

Don't be shocked if you discover the plan's in poor shape or nonexistent. Don't be overly surprised if the objectives aren't clearly stated or if the deliverables are vague and woolly. This type of situation is not as rare as you might think, and it's not the end of the world as long as you take immediate action. Make building a credible plan your top priority.

Barker & Cole's final word on *the art of planning a project* . . .

- When taking on a project think 'Buyer Beware!' Seize the moment to undertake a comprehensive project review.

- Don't strive for the perfect project plan – but do invest time in resolving any critical issues.

- Put the emphasis on what needs to be delivered – rather than what needs to be done.

- When? How much? Don't be bullied into giving crowd-pleasing commitments that are unachievable.

- Sharpen the axe! Make sure you've got a plan you and your team believe in.

Chapter three

risk and
issue
management

transforming admin into action

> **"**Lots of folks confuse bad management with destiny.**"**

Frank McKinney Hubbard (1868–1932)

Introduction

According to a famous Irish bar philosopher, there are three types of people: those who make things happen, those who things happen to, and those who say, 'What happened?'

This homespun, tongue-in-cheek psychology can be accurately extended to project managers. There are those who make sure risks and issues are managed, those who react to events as they happen, and those who say, 'What's happened to my project?' In some cases, project managers who've failed to manage risks and issues will be blissfully unaware of their role in the disaster. Very much like a bad driver whose thoughtlessness causes a motorway pileup and who exhibits innocent amazement at the carnage unfolding in the rear-view mirror.

Even the best managed projects rarely run exactly to plan. Inevitably events will occur that have the potential to derail your project unless they are dealt with effectively. Risk and issue management is a key tool in anticipating and dealing with these events.

It shouldn't happen to a project manager (but it did) . . .

System problems at a large financial institution caused a major outage and loss of revenue, and the proverbial really hit the fan. During the ensuing witch hunt the project manager who recruited the culprit bragged, 'I had my doubts about him at the interview. I asked him about

▶

his weak points and he admitted that he was prone to being careless at times.'

Some people revel in letting everyone know they saw it coming, while conveniently overlooking the consequences of their own inaction.

Managing risks and issues

It's surprising how many people in a project team struggle to define the meaning of 'risk' and 'issue'. In the context of a project:

- a risk is an event that may occur and if it does will threaten the successful delivery of the project;

- an issue is a situation that if left unresolved will have the same effect.

Barker & Cole's world of simple definitions

A **risk** is something bad that might happen; an **issue** is something bad that has happened.

Risk and issue *management* is an approach to anticipating and dealing with events that can cause significant deviations from the project plan. On another level, risk and issue management helps you to pinpoint your plan's weaknesses and gives a useful insight into your project's overall health.

It's more than admin

Considering the importance of risk and issue management, it's disappointing that many project managers see it as a tiresome administrative exercise; a list of extremely unlikely events with dire consequences created at the start of a project. The list – or *log* as it is often called – is immediately filed away in the hope that when things go awry the log can be pulled out with a triumphant shout of, 'I told you so!'

This totally misses the point of the exercise. A brilliant project manager makes risk and issue management something that's revisited repeatedly throughout the project lifecycle.

You know your risks and issues are just there to pad out your project file when ...

■ The project name is incorrect because the list has just been lifted from a previous project.

■ They were last updated on the second day of the project.

■ Everything is at risk, even whether day will follow night.

■ They're kept a closely guarded secret from the rest of the project team.

Process overview

There's a well-established process for handling risk and issues. This is straightforward and involves only three steps:

1 *Identification.* Pinning down the key risks and issues that threaten the success of your project.

2 *Action planning.* Assessing what can be done to deal with them.

3 *Monitoring and control.* Keeping risks and issues under review and adjusting your approach when needed.

It's essential for you to drive this process on behalf of your team. However, any project team member should be encouraged to flag potential issues and risks for assessment. The whole team also has a role to play in seeing through the actions that are agreed.

The risk management process is an iterative one. After the initial identification and assessment of risks and issues have been made, mechanisms should be put in place to keep them under regular review.

This will include looking out for new risks and issues, and reassessing those that have already been captured.

In the remainder of this chapter, we'll explore each step in the process in more depth.

Step 1: identifying key risks and issues

You'll often see risks and issues described in vague and generic terms. A fair number of project managers also treat the identification of risks as a test of their imagination. What unlikely, totally uncontrollable event can they dream up?

Barker & Cole's top tips

Don't spend time worrying about things that are outside of your control. Focus your attention on risks and issues you can influence directly.

A good number of important risks and issues will be immediately apparent – especially to a seasoned project manager. Particularly valuable will be your prior experience of managing similar projects, since many risks and issues are likely to reoccur. As you work with your team to draw up a list of potential risks and issues, it's good to keep three basic questions bubbling away at the back of your mind:

1 *What threats are there to a fit-for-purpose delivery?* This includes concerns about over-engineering as well as falling short of what's required.

2 *What threats are there to keeping to agreed project costs?* Here we're really thinking about overruns since underspend is not that common.

3 *What threats are there to planned delivery timescales?* Again, overrun is the typical concern, since projects don't have a habit of finishing ahead of schedule.

You'll also benefit from some systematic techniques for teasing out those risks and issues that aren't staring you in the face. Once an *risks*

initial pass of the more obvious risks and issues has k
we recommend validating and expanding this list u.
three techniques.

Techniques for identifying risks and issues

1 *Assumptions review.* Consider how safe each important assumption underpinning your plan is.

2 *Lessons learned.* Look at what's gone wrong with other (similar) projects in your neighbourhood.

3 *Checklists.* Work through lists of things to think about and other handy mnemonics.

Assumptions review

Wouldn't it be great to have 20–20 hindsight? Invariably something comes along and temporarily derails your project that seems *fairly obvious* in retrospect. Unfortunately many things that seem obvious after the event aren't that obvious at the time. One excellent way of anticipating problems is by reviewing project assumptions. This is a simple and sensible way of identifying project risks, and perhaps some issues too.

In preparing a project plan, you'll always need to make some assumptions. More often than not, major risks and issues arise when these are misplaced. They also lurk in what are thought to be facts, but turn out to be assumptions in disguise.

Barker & Cole's world of simple definitions

A project **assumption** is more or less anything that has not already happened.

So, first have a careful review of your project *facts* to check they're sound. Then, ask yourself how safe each assumption is. If the answer is something like 'not very', add it to the pile.

Lessons learned

Nearly all risks and issues have hit other projects before. It's one of the few times that you can reap benefit from the suffering of others. If nothing else you'll surely have your own lessons to draw upon.

Not many project managers are keen to own up to or document their mistakes. So you'll be lucky if you find any 'lessons learned' reports. In any event, there's no substitute for simply talking to other project managers and comparing notes. Also people tend to be more candid if the meeting is informal.

For each lesson that you come across, ask yourself whether it applies to your project. If so, add it to your list.

Checklists

When you think you've got a pretty good starting list together, you can use checklists as a prompt to identify additional risks and issues. Checklists provide a series of categories to consider and here's one example:

Schedule	**C**ompatibility
Technology	**L**ifecycle
Organisation	**O**ver-engineering
Resources	**U**sers
Methods	**D**ependencies
	Suppliers

You may be able to find checklists designed with your particular type of project in mind. If you can't lay your hands on any tailored checklists, there's nothing to stop you and your colleagues constructing your own. It's a good way to share your experience.

Risks and issues logs

Once you've got your risks and issues identified, you'll need a place to record them. Logs are used to document specific information about each element. Here's the minimum set of information that we believe you should hold about your risks and issues.

Log item name	Description	Risk log	Issue log
ID	A unique identifier (simply used as a reliable cross-reference)	✓	✓
Raised by	The person who identified the risk or issue	✓	✓
Date raised	The date on which the risk or issue was logged	✓	✓
Description	A clear description of the risk or issue and its impact	✓	✓
Probability	Probability score; the likelihood of a risk occurring	✓	✗
Impact	Impact score; impact on the project of the issue or risk (if the risk occurs)	✓	✓
Score	Risk score; measure of the size of the risk (taking into consideration its likelihood and impact)	✓	✗
Action(s)	The actions agreed to deal with the risk or issue	✓	✓
Owner	The person assigned overall management responsibility and ownership for the risk or issue	✓	✓
Escalate	Whether or not escalation within the organisation is required (yes/no)	✓	✓
Risk/issue x-reference	Cross-reference where an issue has arisen from a previously identified risk	✓	✓
Open/closed	Whether or not the risk or issue is current	✓	✓

There's other information that could be recorded for each risk and issue, but in our experience these are rarely used in a meaningful way. Additional items simply create 'noise' and an unnecessary overhead in maintaining the logs.

One final word of caution: neither too much nor too little! Experience shows that project teams are reluctant to trawl through logs crammed with every risk and issue imaginable. Rather than looking for the gems buried within, they'll simply ignore the logs entirely. So don't allow anything onto your logs unless it really merits attention.

Step 2: action planning

Once you've identified your risks and issues you'll need to plan some positive action, or the whole exercise will have been an interesting but ultimately pointless undertaking. Having picked up a fair number of sick projects in our time, we can't emphasise enough the importance of the old medical adage: prevention is better than cure.

With risks, your first objective is to identify ways of preventing them from happening. These actions are known as *preventative actions*. The key to avoiding risks is simply to ask yourself what could be done to prevent each risk from happening.

For an issue, it's too late to do anything preventative – for that's the very thing that differentiates it from a risk. So instead you have the job of planning actions that can deal with the consequences. These actions are known as *contingent actions* and they should resolve – or at least contain – the issue.

As a further refinement, it's also possible to plan contingent actions for risks. These are the actions that you would take if your preventative measures fail to stop the risk occurring. You could always take the 'I'll cross that bridge when I come to it' approach, but this is not always wise. Fire safety illustrates this nicely. Most offices now employ sensible *preventative* measures to guard against fire; for example making furniture from materials that are not readily combustible. However, *contingent* measures are also usually in place; for example sprinkler systems and rehearsed file drills. Clearly it would be somewhat late in the day to start installing a sprinkler system at the first whiff of smoke.

Prioritising risks and issues

Since risks and issues do not all have the same level of importance, you need to find a way of identifying those that deserve the most attention. There are many ways of doing this, and we've seen many impressively sophisticated means of weighting various factors and calculating scores. However, for most projects, the following simple scoring mechanism provides you with a good way of prioritising risks and issues.

Risk and issue scoring

Risk score = Probability of occurrence $\times$ Impact if risk occurs

Issue score = Impact of issue

There are complex statistical techniques to analyse risk probabilities and to model outcomes. However, we prefer to use the following simple rating system.

Scoring system

Probability of occurrence	**Project impact**
1 – Very unlikely	1 – Negligible
2 – Fairly unlikely	2 – Minor
3 – 50/50 chance	3 – Moderate
4 – Fairly likely	4 – Serious
5 – Almost certain	5 – Disastrous

For example, a risk that was fairly unlikely and would have a serious impact on the project if it occurred would get a risk score of 8 (2 $\times$ 4), while an almost certain risk that carried a moderate impact would get a score of 15 (5 $\times$ 3), and so on.

Having scored your risks and issues using this technique, you can then simply sort them by score. Those with the highest scores deserve your immediate attention.

Step 3: monitoring and control

As we've said, risk and issue management is not something that you just do at the beginning of the project. Quite the contrary: it's something that is part and parcel of day-to-day project management.

It's good practice to incorporate a review of risks and issues as part of tracking project progress. For example, you could make this a standing agenda item at your check-point meetings. You should review both risks and issues already logged, and assess anything new identified by you or your team.

Even a brilliant project manager can't deal single-handedly with each threat to project success. Furthermore, you're unlikely to be best placed to deal with them all directly. However, it's essential that there's always a single point of ownership that can't be passed on. The owner must be actively involved in assessing the relevant risk or issue and agreeing the course of action required.

Barker & Cole's home truths

Key project management tools – such as the risks and issues log – can lose their freshness as quickly as a baguette. If they're not regularly updated they soon become stale.

In some circumstances, resolution of a risk or issue may prove impossible, or it may not be directly within your sphere of influence. If this is the case you must consider escalating resolution to someone more senior. A brilliant project manager is judicious in choosing when to escalate – you don't want to be seen as someone who can't resolve problems. However, there's no point banging your head against a brick wall over resolving matters you simply can't influence.

Most organisations expect appropriate escalation and generally you won't be thanked for holding onto risks and issues that need more senior attention. One important point to note, though, is that use of escalation does not abdicate your responsibility from tracking the risk or issue. A big cheese might have her name against a risk or issue in your log, but that doesn't mean that anything meaningful is being done about it!

Are your logs trying to tell you something?

From time to time, it's a good idea to take a step back to consider your risks and issues logs in their entirety. They provide a useful pointer to the overall health of your project. A large number of significant risks and issues is a sign of a project in trouble. It suggests that more radical action is required than simply trying to address each risk or issue in isolation.

A final tip is to take a look at how the risk and issue logs have evolved over time. As a healthy project progresses, you'd expect that risks would be reduced – or at least contained. You should also see evidence of a good track record in closing down issues. So increasing risk scores, and issues hanging around on the logs indefinitely, should be a cause for concern and further investigation.

Summary

A brilliant project manager won't end up looking around in amazement wondering, 'What happened?' If you manage your risks and issues you'll be giving yourself the best possible chance of side-stepping the avoidable things that threaten your project. Remember: if you don't attack risks and issues they'll attack you!

We know that risk and issue management will never have a glamorous image, but it's often unfairly tagged as a one-off administrative exercise. It's a process that should be applied throughout the project to keep threats firmly in your sights. To do this effectively you need to use a simple, systematic approach so that you don't overlook anything important.

Don't finish your project wishing you'd done a better job of anticipating events and taking early corrective action. Too many project managers end up kicking themselves and wishing '*If only*' because a problem was so obvious with hindsight. With a little extra thought and attention, these risks and issues could have been nipped in the bud.

A brilliant project manager avoids being a victim of chance and circumstance. No doubt you'll have a reputation as someone who makes things happen. But in this context, you'll also be known as someone who makes sure that certain things *don't* happen!

Barker & Cole's final word on *risk and issue management* ...

■ It's not an add-on – it's an intrinsic part of brilliant project management.

■ Your risks and issues should be clear, succinct and above all else specific to your project. Make sure you can see the wood for the trees.

■ A progress review isn't complete without a trawl through your logs.

■ Concentrate your efforts on the biggest risks and issues, not the ones that are easiest to deal with.

■ Use your log to give your project a regular health check.

Chapter four

delivering quality

getting fit for purpose

> **"It's not enough that we do our best,
> sometimes we have to do what's required."**
>
> Sir Winston Churchill (1874–1965)

Introduction

Mention the word 'quality' to some project managers and you'll hear an audible groan. The term comes loaded with connotations of gold-plated solutions, unrealistic customer expectations and misdirected effort.

Project managers understandably respond to the pressure to deliver on time and somewhere close to budget. Quality can often end up as the poor relation to these two very obvious measures of success. However, once the project team has packed up and an organisation has to live with the fruit of its labours, what usually matters most? For the majority of projects, we believe that the quality of delivery is by far the most important dimension.

Imagine you're running a project to build a house and direct most of your attention to timescales and costs. It's unlikely that your customer will say, 'The roof leaks and the foundations are suspect, but the house was finished when you said it would be and you came in on budget. Good job!' However, if quality plays an important part in your plans, the client might say, 'OK, you kept me waiting for two months and it cost me a bit more than I expected, but the house is just what I wanted. For a builder, you've done a pretty good job!' In our experience, the euphoria of an on-time and on-budget delivery is very short-lived if the results are substandard.

You might have heard people talk about the 'cost of quality'. However, we think it's more a case of the 'cost of *no* quality'. You probably know of a piece of work that was carried out as a rushed job to meet some critical deadline, which then turned out to be not so critical when all kinds of problems were found. No doubt considerable time and expense were then expended putting things right. This kind of experience illustrates why compromising on quality is usually counterproductive. Far from being an unnecessary overhead, chasing quality will keep you on track to hand over a solution that delivers lasting customer satisfaction.

You know quality is an irritating point of detail when ...

■ The person responsible for quality on your project was given that role because they didn't seem capable of doing anything else.

■ You rely entirely on an external 'quality team' to make sure what you deliver is up to the job.

■ Quality checks are put on the 'only do if time left' list – behind organising the end-of-project party.

What does quality mean?

The term quality means many things to many people. Sometimes it's used in the 'gold-plated' sense we referred to in the opening of this chapter. However, for a project we apply a more pragmatic definition: meeting expectations and requirements.

Plumbing in the hotel industry provides us with a neat way of illustrating this slant on quality! Say we have the job of supplying taps to one of the finest hotels in the world, which is seeking to attract customers who are used to the finest things in life. The specification for the taps would include practical things like the ability to turn on and off, and long-term reliability. Being a very upmarket hotel, gold plating or some other sign of opulence would also be essential. Now imagine that we're supplying taps to a budget chain of hotels. The ability to turn on and off, and reliability, would still be relevant requirements – but the requirement for any luxurious embellishment would be an expensive frivolity.

So, in our world, quality hinges on what extent something is *fit for the purpose for which it is intended* – not that it has any special worth or extra degree of refinement. In fact, by our definition, both over-engineered and under-engineered solutions are poor quality. Ultimately this requires a good understanding of what the customer *needs*, not just what the customer *wants*.

Barker & Cole's world of simple definitions

Quality is all about delivering something that's fit for the purpose for which it's intended.

Agreeing what's fit-for-purpose

The biggest problem with the pursuit of quality is in making it a tangible, measurable concept. After all, how can you be expected to deliver quality if it's specified in vague terms? Delivering something that's of *good quality* or *appropriate quality* is as difficult as clapping with one hand.

We know from experience that it can be difficult to reach agreement as to what fit-for-purpose really means. This is because a project manager may well disagree with the customer's view of what's essential. This isn't to say you shouldn't be prepared to debate the necessity of their requirements, but you must remember that ultimately it's the customer's final decision as to how fitness for purpose is specified.

Getting a clear and reliable definition of what constitutes fit-for-purpose on your project is crucial for its success. We therefore want to take a closer look at exactly what we mean by *fit-for-purpose* in the project context. Much hinges on reaching a reasonable agreement with your customer about the essence of what is needed.

Barker & Cole's home truths

Poor quality leaves behind a bitter taste that lingers longer than the warm glow generated by achieving a tight deadline or a cheap price.

Fit-for-purpose baseline

Put simply, your objective is to deliver your project with your *customers* accepting that what you've supplied is fit for its intended purpose. To achieve this you'll need to agree a specific set of deliverables before you start work. This needs to be more than just a simple list and should be a rich description of all of the important features.

It's usually difficult to establish the fine detail of what's required for a project – especially in the early stages. Your first attempts to nail down what the customer wants are likely to be sprinkled with extra features that can't be accurately claimed as essential. Your role is to help your customers to sort out the genuinely mandatory (the must-haves) from the really important and nice-to-haves.

A useful technique for steering your customers through this discussion is to introduce some kind of prioritisation. You can then let your customers list everything, even the bells and whistles, as long as they attach their rating of how essential each item is. The next step is to work with them to agree which are *absolutely essential* for the project to meet its objectives.

Reaching a perfect agreement isn't a reasonable expectation: it's not necessary either. As long as the specification isn't inundated with superfluous extras, there's no problem with accepting a few extra treats. It's far better to let a couple of extra features creep in – even if you're convinced they're not entirely necessary – as long as the bulk of the requirements are pitched correctly. After all, in the end it's your customers' call as to what's deemed essential and what's not.

The resulting mandatory requirements equip you with a *minimum fit-for-purpose baseline*. As a brilliant project manager, you'll want to deliver considerably more than this.

Fit-for-purpose baseline top tips

- *Ensure the people who agree the quality baseline are also involved in the project sign-off.* This will achieve a consistent view on what's fit-for-purpose.

- *The definition of a mandatory requirement is that if it's not met, the whole delivery has to be rejected.* Use this acid test to encourage your customers to be reasonable about what's listed as essential.

- *Agree the relative priority of optional add-ons.* Treats aren't of equal importance and you may have to sacrifice some in favour of others.

- *Help your customers to understand the cost of items that are of marginal benefit.* Encourage them to consider dropping anything that's poor value.

- *Anything included in the fit-for-purpose baseline is non-negotiable.* If time or cost pressures become acute, some treats will have to be dropped.

Negotiating around quality

One of the biggest problems you'll face is an inflated set of mandatory requirements – in fact this happens on nearly every project. It's not unknown for everything to become essential. This distorts the definition of what fit-for-purpose means, and increases costs and timescales. It also removes scope for manoeuvre if times get tough, because too many treats are seen as non-discretionary.

Sometimes this happens innocently, when customers confuse what they'd *like* with what they really *need*. Other times, the reasons are more calculated. Keep an eye out for typical problems in this area:

- *Lack of experience in stating what's needed.* There's a good chance that the people responsible for providing requirements will be doing this without much experience. So they'll need some guidance on how they should go about describing what they need. They'll also need to understand the implications of loading on requirements that aren't strictly necessary.

- *Different perspectives from the top and bottom.* Most projects have to serve a variety of masters, striking a balance between achieving high-level goals and delivering something useful for people working at the coal face. People at an operational level tend to overstate what they can't live without and more senior personnel tend to see too many things as just nice-to-have.

■ *Taking a negotiating position.* Given that most projects are known to falter in one way or another, many customers anticipate their project will fall short of whatever's agreed up-front. Therefore they (craftily) overstate their requirements, so they can be negotiated back to where they wanted to be in the first place.

Whatever the reason, it's important to coax customers back into realistic definitions of what they really need and what they'd like. Facilitate a meaningful discussion on this and try to tease out the facts. However, remember that it's the customer, not you, who makes the final call on what fit-for-purpose means for a project. Accept that the interpretation of quality inevitably involves some degree of subjectivity. After all, you won't be able to persuade the owners of Dubai's seven-star Burj Al Arab Hotel – reputedly the most luxurious in the world – that lavish bathroom fittings are a nice-to-have optional extra!

It shouldn't happen to a project manager (but it did) . . .

The explanation of the importance of prioritising requirements went down extremely well with one receptive customer: 'This is a much better way of doing things.' The project manager approached the rating of the requirements list with confidence. She started at the top and worked her way down. The first requirement was rated as a 'mandatory'. This was quickly followed by 'mandatory' for the second. And the third, and so on, until all the requirements were universally rated as essential and non-negotiable. The customer was delighted with the requirements prioritisation exercise.

Like giving up a bad habit, it's easier to gain agreement to the theory than to put it into practice.

Measuring quality

There's an old saying that 'if you can't measure it, you can't manage it'. On a project, if you have some clear and well-thought-out measures for assessing what's fit-for-purpose, it's going to be easier to spot things going wrong and to act accordingly. So how do you go about doing this?

Our starting point is that a project's success will largely be assessed by the things it *delivers*, rather than the activities it *does* to deliver. So, quality measures must focus on project outputs. These include both the final deliverables and any intermediate ones that are required along the way.

The most basic question is whether all of the planned deliverables have been produced. The next level of assessment is to take a close look at what's been produced to see whether they conform to specification. A great way to do this is to use *quality criteria*. These are tests that should be applied to a deliverable to see whether it's fit-for-purpose.

We recommend you phrase your quality criteria as succinct and specific questions. These will encourage an objective and focused assessment of what's been produced. For example: 'Have the foundations been dug to sufficient depth to support the planned two-storey building?'

Quality criteria should be defined up-front as part of specifying a project deliverable. That way, the people who are working on your project will know how their efforts will be assessed. This in turn increases the probability that what they turn out will be fit-for-purpose.

Barker & Cole's top tips

When you're defining your quality criteria, don't just think short term. It's easy to overlook some of the things that might matter once the project has been wrapped up. For example, you might want quality criteria to check the ease of maintenance once the project team has been disbanded.

Quality reviews

A key principle of project quality control is that measures are taken at frequent intervals – *especially* early on. It's essential to reduce the cost of any rework by intercepting problems when they'll be both easier and cheaper to correct. Bizarrely many projects never have enough time to get things right first time, but always find enough time to do it all over again.

As a general rule, we recommend you arrange three quality reviews during the production of any important deliverable:

- *Before anyone even starts work.* Get the key players together to review the specification of the deliverable and the quality criteria that will be used to assess its fitness for purpose. It's amazing how much misunderstanding and ambiguity this uncovers. Far better to have a hand-wringing session before work starts, than trying to rectify a major misunderstanding once work is well under way.

- *At the earliest point during construction when the first sensible measure of quality can be taken.* This is an ideal opportunity not only to check that things are heading in the right direction but also to clear up any outstanding issues in connection with the deliverable specification or its quality criteria.

- *As development of a deliverable is completed or is nearing completion.* A final checkpoint that will, hopefully, reveal only minor deviations from specification. If major deficiencies are uncovered at least they're known about sooner rather than later.

If the deliverable passes its quality review, work can proceed as planned. If the deliverable falls short, you'll need to agree the rework required and then make sure that this is incorporated in the project schedule.

One tip is to arrange for quality reviews to be built into the flow of work. There are usually several points in a project where deliverables are handed over like the baton in a relay race. At each of these hand-over points we recommend the deliverable is verified as fit-for-purpose by whoever is on the receiving end of the delivery. This person will have a vested interest in ensuring the quality is right and this is their best opportunity to draw attention to any flaws.

It shouldn't happen to a project manager (but it did) ...

One project team introduced metrics into its quality control process and started rating each delivery to track quality trends. All went well for a time. The metrics provided a useful tool for spotting problems early. Then suddenly the metrics indicated a sharp and unexpected decline in one area. After investigation by the project manager, it transpired that a few individuals were using the marking system to settle personal vendettas. They were routinely marking deliveries from certain of their colleagues harshly – no matter how good the quality of the work.

Quality reviews are like knives: useful devices but dangerous weapons in the wrong hands. Make sure they're always objective and constructive.

Right people, right skills, write quality

It's totally counterproductive to receive misleading feedback – be that misguided and irrelevant critiques, or a glowing bill of health that subsequently proves misplaced. To find out how well your project is *really* doing you'll need to ensure that the right people undertake your quality reviews.

Be sure that you get the right match between the reviewer's skills and experience and the type of review being requested. For example, a common pitfall is to provide a customer with a document to review that's full of jargon. Then when things fall apart they'll say that it seemed OK to them at the time, but they weren't really sure what they were looking at.

It's the project manager's responsibility to make sure that either deliverables are presented in a way that matches the reviewer's skills and experience, or some practical help is given during the review process by someone who can highlight and explain the most important review points.

Encouraging a thorough review

Having got the right people involved, it's essential to ensure each reviewer is thorough and doesn't resort to a quick run through. People tend to be busy and don't always devote enough time to the task. This leads to vague comments like 'it looks alright to me' or even worse the dreaded 'nil-return'. The value of a review is directly proportional to the effort put in and gentle cajoling will pay dividends.

Implementing a degree of formality to reviewing deliverables, particularly documents, is a good way of encouraging thorough reviews. The key is to ask for a sign-off as this creates a different mindset for the reviewer. Consider the two following options for requesting a document review:

1 'Can you give this a look over and let me know if you spot anything wrong. If I don't hear from you, I'll assume it's OK.'

2 'I need your review of this report using the attached comments sheet and sign-off by email. Once it's signed off it will be baselined and any subsequent changes will be subject to our change control procedures.'

The first brief will probably result in a cursory glance; the latter is more likely to result in a thorough review of the document.

Barker & Cole's top tips

Even if a review is undertaken through correspondence, try to get everyone together for a final run through of comments received. Interaction will help flush out any issues and put maximum pressure on each reviewer to perform an active review.

The people producing the deliverables must always be involved in the review process to ensure everyone understands the outcome. All points raised during a review must be acted on or there must be a solid reason why not.

It's also a good idea to agree the relative importance of the problems and issues that are identified. This will enable the project team to invest its time in fixing what really matters, rather than being diverted to superfluous fine-tuning. However this is one occasion where we like to see a degree of pedantic criticism (e.g. highlighting grammatical errors in a written document) as long as this is not the only type of comment received. It tells you that the reviewers have been paying attention!

External assurance

Although you'll always want to see the pursuit of quality integrated into your projects, it's wise to consider additional quality assurance checks run by people outside of the team. In fact, within some organisations or industries external reviews are a mandatory requirement.

A fresh pair of eyes on a project is always a welcome addition. Scheduling external quality assurance checks also encourages you to take a step back from the day-to-day whirlwind of management and take another look at intrinsic quality with the help of an independent viewpoint. Even if no formal assurance team is available, you could always ask another experienced individual you respect to provide an informal review of your project.

Sometimes formal assurance points will be predetermined. If not, you'll have to decide where they'll be most effective. The key to this is to identify the largest 'pinch points' in the project. The litmus test for any assurance point is to think about where the effort is most likely to be outweighed by the cost of not undertaking the review.

Factors to consider when you're planning your external assurance points

- *Mandated assurance points.* Are any assurance points mandated within the organisation or industry? If not, are there any industry best practices for assurance that provide a useful pointer?

- *Points of 'no return'.* Are there any points where the consequences of having to backtrack, now or at a later date, would be serious?

- *Points where funds are committed.* Are there any scheduled payments or other financial commitments? What checks should be made *before* funds are committed?

- *Natural break points.* Most projects consist of a number of distinct phases. Are any of these break points a useful place to take an assurance review?

As with internal reviews, the value of any external quality assurance review depends on the skills and experience of the reviewers involved. Unfortunately many organisations seem to have a policy of using quality assurance departments as a retirement home for individuals whom they believe have outlived their usefulness anywhere else. Nevertheless a positive attitude to working with an assurance team can pay dividends. They're often unfairly maligned, just like project managers!

Summary

Issues with timescales and costs are easy to spot and therefore get immediate attention. Shortcomings in quality are not always as obvious and can lurk beneath the surface. Often they emerge only when the final delivery is rejected by the customer, having been labelled as substandard.

Your customers will judge your project by whether what it delivers is fit-for-purpose. It's important to agree what's mandatory for the project and translate this into a baseline that defines what's truly non-negotiable. You'll also need to help customers pin down what they'd *like* the project to deliver and to encourage them not to over-inflate their essential requirements.

Brilliant project managers know the cost of failing to meet customer expectations. They also recognise it's far more cost-effective to invest effort up-front to prevent this from happening in the first place, rather than dealing with the consequences of handing over something that's not up to the job.

Brilliant project managers also realise that their long-term reputation stands or falls on what they deliver. So, unless you're planning on putting on your running shoes the day before your project delivers, work with your customers to define quality and make achieving this your primary goal.

Barker & Cole's final word on *delivering quality* ...

- Quality doesn't have to be a vague, intangible concept. Define what fit-for-purpose means in specific and measurable terms.

- Be prepared to accept that your customers have the final word on the difference between what they want and what they really need.

- Build quality reviews into your daily routine. Check your deliverables are fit-for-purpose at every step along the way.

▶

- Be open to the contribution that an external quality assurance team could make.

- There's no point in delivering something that no-one wants – even if this is achieved quickly or cheaply. Never let time and cost pressures compromise your minimum fit-for-purpose baseline.

Chapter five

resource management

from estimating to completing

> **❝I have no money, no resources and no hopes.
> I am the happiest man alive.❞**

Henry Miller (1891–1980)

Introduction

One of the biggest myths around is that project managers regularly deliver on time and within budget, successfully managing all their resources with only minor hiccups en route. Not surprisingly, it's mainly project managers themselves spinning this tall tale, with the phrase 'on time and to budget' featuring heavily in their CVs.

Fortunately, project management hocus-pocus is not protected by the Magic Circle, otherwise we couldn't reveal that this is often just a clever sleight of hand. Yes, let's put our cards on the table: many projects overrun in some way, ending up delivered late or over budget.

What *is* surprising though is the somewhat defeatist attitude some organisations take towards project costs and timescales. Perhaps because projects consistently overrun, some customers attempt damage limitation by insisting on starting with the lowest number possible, however optimistic. This is in the forlorn hope that they can use this opening gambit to constrain the final outcome.

Even within organisations that seem to take a lenient view of missed deadlines or blown budgets, brilliant project managers prefer to take a rigorous approach to resource management. They find this makes life easier because projects that are in good shape are easier to manage. Conversely, they know that spiralling costs and receding completion dates would undermine general confidence in their ability to deliver.

Dealing with low expectations

When an organisation readily accepts slipped deadlines and cost over-runs – and such places aren't as rare as you might think – it's easy to slip into the same easy-going rut. At first it's a good life. There's a relaxed attitude to delivery and everyone works with the urgency of the day-after-mañana. However you'll find that your project becomes steadily more difficult to run.

Soon it becomes clear how time consuming and ultimately frustrating it is to constantly replan. Eventually it becomes tempting to give up any semblance of management and let the project deliver itself. Which, of course, is a recipe for disaster! It's much more productive when your effort is invested in planning, organising and tracking resources, rather than constantly reacting to one crisis after another.

So, even if you're working in an easy-going place where nobody gets hot under the collar about deadlines and budgets, don't simply fall into line behind your colleagues. However others are behaving, it's still important for you to have a good grip on resource management.

It's not only about money

Resource management is not just focused on money; it's about all kinds of resources, especially people. It's about knowing what resources are needed to complete a project. It's also about managing those resources to bring about a successful delivery. This includes understanding lead times, identifying bottlenecks and arranging for resources to be in the right place at the right time.

Barker & Cole's world of simple definitions

Resource management is the art of knowing what resources you need to deliver successfully and then getting the best out of them.

Resource planning is an integral part of your overall *project* planning. You can't manage your project if you're not managing your resources.

In the remainder of this chapter we'll take a look at tools and techniques for managing project resources, starting with the first job of preparing estimates.

Don't underestimate the importance of estimating

Estimating is at the heart of resource planning. You'll be using estimates to arrive at your best prediction of the resources required to deliver your project. You'll need to know both the types and quantities of these resources. A brilliant project manager will also have a good feel for how reliable these estimates are.

Before we look at *how* to prepare estimates, it's worth considering *who* should provide them. As with other aspects of planning, the golden rule is to involve the people who'll be doing the actual work, but don't simply leave them to their own devices. You'll need to guide them in this task to get the quality of estimate you're after.

When it's not possible to prepare estimates with the people who'll be doing the work, you'll need to identify who's best placed to help you with this task. Unless you really understand the detail, don't simply produce the figures yourself. If you take this shortcut, you'll end up with an educated guess rather than an estimate, and it will probably all end in tears.

Barker & Cole's top tips

When you need an estimate, ask for optimistic and pessimistic figures. This gets people thinking. An average of the two numbers is a reasonable starting point for your estimate.

Estimating accuracy

Estimates produced in the early days of projects are prone to be inaccurate. Initial predictions can be out by a factor of 200–300%. Typically, the precision of estimates will improve throughout the course of the project.

Before launching into a resource estimating exercise, it's important to establish the level of accuracy you want to achieve – and whether it's really achievable. For example, if you're involved in preparing a bid for a fixed-price project, you'll want to have a relatively high degree of confidence in your quote. If, on the other hand, you've been asked to provide an early ballpark figure that can be refined later on, you might be able to live with a minimum–maximum range.

The level of accuracy required determines how much time you'll need to invest in the estimating exercise. No matter how much effort you put in, the results will not be sufficiently accurate if they're based on vague requirements. So if you need tight, reliable estimates, you also need clearly defined and *agreed* requirements. If you're after a *starter for ten*, it's not necessary to pin down requirements to the same degree.

At this point, a word of caution is needed. Customers have a habit of seizing on ballpark figures and then immediately treating them as fixed-cost commitments. Or similarly, only the lower end of a range of costs sticks in their minds. You'll also find that any assumptions, attached conditions or caveats are somewhat conveniently forgotten. It's no wonder projects overrun in these circumstances.

A brilliant project manager must hammer home any assumptions and caveats. Having been burned when a minimum–maximum range is quoted, we favour budgeting on the basis of the upper end of the estimate. There's often initially a drawback with this approach – a sharp intake of breath from the customer – but longer term, there's less likelihood of disappointment.

Barker & Cole's home truths

Estimates are normally quoted with a plus and minus percentage. The minus option never materialises.

Estimating techniques

The best estimating techniques to use will be dependent upon the specifics of your project and the field you're working in. For some projects, sophisticated estimating tools will be available. For others, gut feel and prior experience will play more of a role. But, whatever kind of project you're responsible for, we'd recommend you work through the following process.

1   *Determine how you want your resource estimates organised and presented.* In particular, organisations often have standard resource categories that a project manager needs to follow. For example, it's common to find that costs need to be broken down by capital and operating expenditure at least; and people resources by specific job roles.

2   *Break up the estimating exercise into manageable chunks.* Your estimators will find it easier to provide meaningful resource estimates if they are presented with bite-sized pieces of work to consider. Try to relate these units of work to specific project deliverables.

3   *Get estimates for each piece of work.* Make sure you know how the estimators arrived at their figures and that you're happy with any assumptions they've used along the way.

4   *Produce your summary estimate.* Aggregate the estimates for the various pieces of work, to provide an overall resource projection. Highlight any key assumptions that have been used.

5   *Validate your estimates.* Check your figures by finding at least one other way of arriving at resource estimates for your project. For example, compare this project to a previous one that's similar. You could also get an independent review from another project manager.

Common estimating pitfalls

Whether you've got a sophisticated estimating tool or are using the back of an envelope, there are some common pitfalls that are just waiting to trip you up as you prepare your resource estimates. Keep an eye out for the following.

Top estimating tripwires

- Bowing to pressure to replace carefully estimated figures with more palatable numbers provided by someone senior.

- Treating the project scope as fixed and agreed when it's woolly and not signed off.

- Thinking that estimates inherited from someone else are rigorously researched and carefully calculated.

- Taking estimates provided by project team members at face value. Not factoring in excessive caution or optimism – or perhaps simple inexperience.

- Missing out chunks of work completely or not understanding all the steps required to complete a task.

- Estimating the effort required from highly skilled people, when a mixed-ability team is actually going to do the work.

Building resource contingency

At the start of a project it's not possible to fix what will be delivered, how long it will take *and* how much it will cost. The best you can hope for is to set one or two of these in concrete. For example, you could fix the costs and timescales but vary what you deliver to fit within those constraints. Alternatively, you could fix the deliverables and vary the time and cost.

Resource contingency is something that's added to estimates to guard against things requiring more work than expected or simply to reflect the fact that an estimate isn't that reliable. Contingency is usually built into individual work packages or added *en bloc* to one or more general pots.

It's common to incorporate contingency at both levels. Understanding how much is already built into individual, detailed estimates is part of deciding how much additional contingency you should allow for the project as a whole.

Work package contingency

The first kind of contingency is about ensuring realism regarding the amount of effort required to complete each individual piece of work. Depending on the nature of the work involved and who's prepared the estimates, you might add varying levels of contingency to selected work packages. Optimistic Oliver who's been looking at a risky piece of work might get a 50% loading on his resource estimates, while nothing is added to Cautious Caroline's estimate for repeating a bit of work that's already a known quantity.

This kind of contingency gives you a more realistic resource estimate for completing your project, on the basis that each individual work package within the overall project proceeds broadly to plan.

Pots of contingency

More general contingency is added to deal with significant events that could impact on your project. For example, an unfortunate misunderstanding about scope might be uncovered. This contingency is usually placed in a central pot, but it can be held in other ways such as by resource type or project stage.

Your contingency will often be challenged by your customers or whoever is paid to worry about the costs. If cutbacks are proposed, you need to be prepared to explain why the contingency is needed and what the implications would be if it is taken away.

> **Barker & Cole's home truths**
>
> Customers have short-term memories when it comes to removing contingency. When you can't keep on track they'll forget they left you with no room to manoeuvre.

You should review your contingency as the project progresses. This involves accounting for any contingency that's been used and reviewing what you need for the rest of the project. As a healthy project unfolds, contingency levels should go down.

Use your contingency wisely

When a task is handed out it must be accompanied by an estimate. However, if you include the contingency from the beginning, you'll find that the work expands to fill the time allocated and the cushion will be immediately lost. This 'wriggle room' should be used only if things don't go according to plan. Sometimes it won't be needed, sometimes it will, and sometimes it won't be enough. Overall, you can expect the use of contingency to even out over time.

Your central contingency funds should be used only once you've exhausted all other options. They should be used for managing significant adverse events – but not for outright catastrophes. For example, if you discover your customer is expecting a fully carpeted house for the price quoted, you could meet the additional costs out of your general contingency funds. On the other hand, if you find that the house has a major structural problem, you'll need to deal with this as a major project *exception*.

Preparing a resource schedule

Once you've got to the point of having estimated what kinds of resources are required to deliver your project and how much of each type of resource is needed, you're ready to start building a resource schedule.

Your resource schedule is all about making sure that you get your resources in the right place at the right time. This might sound simple, but there's quite an art to this – especially when you take into account that it's unlikely everything will go according to plan.

A resource schedule describes how much of each resource you intend to use over time. You can think of it as a table with a row for each resource type and a column for each week or month of your project. Each table cell will record how much resource you plan to use for that resource type, in that week or month.

Example: an excerpt from Rob the Builder's resource schedule . . .

	Month 1	Month 2	Month 3	Month 4	Month 5
Capital costs					
Digger	–	£10,000	–	–	–
Expenses					
Architect fees	£5,000	£2,000	–	–	£2,000
Materials	£1,000	£10,000	£5,000	£2,000	£2,000
People					
Labourers	1	2	4	4	4
Carpenters	–	2	–	1	–
Plasterers	–	–	–	–	2

By looking down a column, you can use your schedule to show what particular resources you'll need in any given period. Each row also provides a picture of how a type of resource gets used over time.

There's a close relationship between your resource schedule and your project schedule. In fact they need to be developed in tandem since one doesn't make sense without the other. Most planning tools will help you to generate the resource schedule.

In particular, project managers know that resourcing constraints will have an important influence on timelines. This is a fact that's overlooked by some who come unstuck after publishing a schedule

...ly then start to think about how the project is going to be

A difficult balancing act

In preparing a resource schedule there are trade-offs to be made between resources and timescales. While remaining committed to supplying something that's fit-for-purpose, a project manager needs to strike the right balance between the cost of delivery and the time required to achieve this. Typically, constraining resources is likely to lengthen timescales and vice versa. Barker & Cole's quality see-saw illustrates this trade-off:

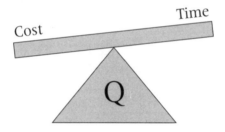

With quality remaining pivotal, if you put pressure on costs you can expect timescales to go up and when you put pressure on timescales, costs go up.

Your starting point is to understand your customer's priorities. Often they'll have a particular delivery date in mind and sometimes they'll put specific constraints on the budget. Using these priorities you're looking to get the optimum balance between resources and timescales. You may need to discuss some of the options with your customers. Make sure you get beyond the idea that they want your project to be both cheap and quick!

Book early to avoid disappointment

A brilliant project manager is always forward thinking to ensure resources are on hand when needed. This involves making an early booking and reconfirming availability nearer to the planned start date.

Inevitably things will not always go according to plan and a project manager must deal with unexpected changes in resource availability. This is especially true where people are concerned, for example when they're delayed on another assignment. Be ready to work around these problems, but avoid the temptation to reassign work to whoever happens to be available. If you use the wrong type of resource for a job, it's a recipe for rework.

Always keep a close eye on resources that are in high demand compared with their availability. This might be an expert with a particular set of valuable skills or some equipment that has limited capacity. You might have to base at least part of your resource schedule around the availability of these resources.

Barker & Cole's home truths

Regular overtime and weekend working by week two of a project is a sure sign that the resource schedule doesn't stack up.

Even when you book ahead you may run into resource bottlenecks. If that happens look again to see whether there's an alternative resource that you could use. Also investigate whether there's a way of reordering the work to smooth out your resource demands.

Lead times and ramp-up

It can be easy to overlook the time it takes to get resources on board and fully effective. However, these two things have undone many resource schedules. *Lead time* is the time that it takes to get a resource on board. *Ramp-up* is the time it takes for a resource to be fully effective.

Lead times might range from a couple of days for recruiting an internal team member to weeks for an external consultant or even months for a new product to be procured by a government department. Sometimes it's not just the type of resource that matters but how much you need. You might be able to source one expert with some niche skills in a few days but if you need a dozen of them you could be searching for weeks or months. It's essential that you make a realistic assessment of the lead times for each of your resources and then build this into your resource schedule.

You must also allow for the fact that, once a resource arrives, it's unlikely to be fully effective from day one. The most common example is the need to induct a new team member, but ramp-up time also extends to things like equipment commissioning, software installation and office facility set-up.

When looking at inducting new team members, it's important that you also account for the time that will be lost to existing team members as they spend time bringing the new arrivals up to speed. Be careful not to underestimate this effort – it can be considerable.

Avoiding resource overload

A brilliant project manager won't start off with a resource schedule in which all the resources are fully loaded for the duration they're used, especially people. This is because resources rarely operate at their full capacity.

Be sure that you understand how much effective time you can *really* expect from your team members. By the time holiday, training, sickness and socialising are taken into account, somebody assigned to you full-time might average only the equivalent of four days' work a week at best. So if your resource estimates suggest you require a team of five people, in reality you're probably in need of six or seven.

However keen you are on sweating your resources, there are things a brilliant project manager must factor into a realistic resource plan:

- *Official and unofficial public holidays.* If you are running a multi-national project, don't forget that these holidays vary considerably around the world.

- *Booked leave or unplanned leave.* Check who's going on holiday and when. Include a pro-rata allowance each week or month if firm dates are not available.

- *Sick leave and training.* Make a realistic allowance to cover sick leave and training.

- *Admin and other overheads.* Nearly all jobs entail a degree of non-project-related admin and non-productive tasks. Don't underestimate the time that these can take.

Resource tracking

Once you've worked hard on your resource schedule and your project is under way, it's important to track actual against planned resource usage. Not just because you ought to know how much your project has cost, but to help you to refine your resource plan going forward.

Most people have a natural tendency to want to please and may just tell you what they think you'd like to hear rather than what's really happening. It's essential that you have plenty of contact with your team members, even if this is informal. That way, you'll be able to compare official news on progress with what you can see happening for yourself.

Your *actual* against *planned* resource usage should feature as a standard item in your progress reports. An interesting point to note is that spending less than forecast is not necessarily a good sign. This could mean that work is not starting on time and this might be an early warning that you're falling behind schedule.

Completion is everything

A brilliant project manager keeps a close eye on what the resources used to date have actually *achieved*. Our motto here is: 'Progress is of interest. But completion is everything.'

You've probably had experience of a task that seemed to be progressing well, with its owner confidently reporting a rapidly increasing percentage complete figure – until about 90% complete is reached. At this point, progress gets stuck at around the 90% mark – week after week.

There's a danger in relying on *percentage complete* as a measure of progress. People tend to be over-optimistic about what it takes to finish off the last pieces of outstanding work, which are usually the most problematic. Instead, measure progress in terms of what's been *finished*. And you need to make sure that 'finished' means that absolutely no more work needs to be done. Again, people have a habit of glossing over the outstanding finishing touches and are prone to saying something is complete when it isn't.

Barker & Cole's home truths

If a task is described as 'about 90% complete', it doesn't necessarily mean that it's close to being finished.

Reporting on finished work *only* is a much more accurate way to measure progress, although at times it will appear that nothing's getting done. However, there's no risk of myriad nearly finished tasks falsely creating an impression of significant progress.

Measuring outstanding work

A useful technique for providing a warning of extra work is to ask your team to report on the outstanding cost to complete. The key principle here is that the amount of outstanding work is a much better indicator of progress than the effort you've spent to date. Let's illustrate this with an example.

You're told that a task is going to take ten days' effort to complete and that four days will be spent on that task this week.

At the end of the week, you ask for a progress update and are told:

■ three days were spent working on the task;

■ there are eight days of outstanding work remaining.

So you now know that:

- only three days out of the planned four days were spent on the task; and

- only two days of productive work were actually achieved (since this is the amount by which the outstanding work has been reduced).

These metrics are a valuable source of information about project progress. First, they tell you whether resources are being used according to plan. Second, and crucially, they tell you whether you're getting through the work at the rate you forecast.

Summary

You'll be remembered primarily for the quality of what you deliver, but this doesn't mean that you can sit back and adopt a casual approach to resources and timescales. Your customers will certainly attach great importance to keeping within budget. For your own benefit, sound resource management leads to a far more productive and less frustrating day at the office.

You'll be able to trace much of your success here back to a well thought out resource schedule and flexibility in dealing with changing circumstances. The final ingredient is using completion as a true measure for tracking progress.

It would be dishonest to pretend that it's unusual for projects to overrun in some way – whether taking longer or spending more than planned. It's usually because resource management has been poor. So if you want to keep your customers satisfied, and you're looking for an easy life, don't loosen your grip on project resources.

Barker & Cole's final word on *resource planning and management* ...

- Whatever others are doing, set your own gold standard for rigorous resource management.

- Estimates are the bedrock of resource management. Get these wrong and you'll be building on quicksand.

- Contingency is your lifeline – retain control over it and use it wisely.

- Book your resources well in advance and confirm your reservation before the start date.

- Make sure your expectations of productivity are realistic. Even the best workers go on holiday and occasionally pause for a chat with their colleagues.

- Be sceptical about reports of progress. Demand to see the *finished* goods!

Chapter six

leading
effective
teams

making the most of your
assets

Introduction

If you can't work well with people you'll never be a brilliant project manager. So much of a project's success revolves around how the people in a team perform – and a project manager plays a pivotal role in this. Project management isn't simply a technical discipline conducted in some dark corner. A large part of the role involves building effective working relationships with a whole range of people – and sometimes in challenging circumstances. A mantra for us is: project managers manage *people* not activities.

There's a prevalent view that managers don't need to be popular; that in fact they're more effective if their teams don't like them. Autocratic, dictatorial, kick-up-the-backside project managers have lived by this philosophy for many years. For some, this has brought considerable success. But success built on trepidation is short-lived and rarely repeatable. We agree that project management isn't a popularity contest. However, as a project manager you won't be brilliant without the respect and support of your team and other key individuals around you.

For us, the litmus test for project managers is whether or not they can repeat success. Whether or not they can repeatedly build effective teams – sometimes using personnel regarded as average performers. For this to happen, you must develop a reputation based on respect – respect for your knowledge of the job and how you carry out your role. You also need to possess at least a core set of likeable characteristics!

It shouldn't happen to a project manager (but it did) ...

A cynical employee we came across was not a big fan of project managers, yet was heard purring with delight about a new recruit. What was the secret to this unparalleled turnaround? The new sheriff in town brought doughnuts to the weekly team meetings!

Small tokens can make a big impression. It's amazing how productive a simple gesture can be.

Start with a smile

Quite often teams have low expectations where the behaviour of their managers is concerned. Therefore simple displays of good manners are a fine start. You'd be amazed how productive cheerful 'good morning' and 'good night' salutes are. It's very simple and surprisingly effective. Make sure you're polite to everyone though, not only the movers, shakers and beautiful people.

Of course, it takes more than a cheerful 'hello' in the morning to get your team firing on all cylinders. There are many effective techniques that are simple to use and we've grouped them into three topics:

- *Building a project team* – recruiting and inducting new team members.
- *Motivating the team* – techniques for improving your team's productivity.
- *Providing leadership* – setting direction and building a loyal following.

Barker & Cole's home truths

First impressions count. If you get off to a poor start with your team, it's very hard to recover confidence and support.

Building your project team

Project managers rarely inherit a fully fledged and effective team. More often than not they inherit one that's already misfiring or they have to start by building from scratch. The practical constraints you'll encounter when assembling your team will make this a challenging task. Some of the following might sound familiar:

- *Budget constraints preventing much-needed recruiting.* Or conversely a generous budget fuelling unrealistic expectations of a fast ramp-up.

- *Projects being used as a dumping ground.* Other managers using your new team as a convenient home for staff that they're not really sure what to do with.

- *Selfish managers who monopolise the best staff.* They hold onto the star performers even when their skills and experience are desperately needed elsewhere.

All this is invariably against a backdrop of an acute sense of urgency to get a team up and running. It's essential not to be panicked into making rash decisions. Building the right team – as far as it's realistic – is one of the factors critical to the success of any project. Avoid the temptation to recruit indiscriminately or to think anybody is better than nobody.

Team recruitment

It's essential to have a controlled approach to recruiting, making sure you always have the right people on tap when they're needed. Your recruitment activity should be driven by your resource schedule and your expected lead times. Whatever happens, don't miss out a key stage in your project just because the right resources aren't on board. It's surprising how many projects commit *hara-kiri* by starting the main building works before the foundations are laid, just because the right resources weren't on hand when needed.

Team recruitment tips

■ *Make recruiting key team members a priority.* In the very early stages of a project it can be tempting to put off recruitment activity. However, without a team in place you're never going to deliver. So give serious consideration to clearing the decks for team recruitment – even if this means some short-term pain.

■ *Take an objective and constructive look at the staff on offer.* Be wary of second-hand assessments of personnel on offer. Form your own views on their capabilities and the extent to which they meet your requirements. Remember that many so-called under-achievers flourish in a project environment when given the right direction and support.

■ *Think about the mix of people that will work well together.* You're unlikely to need a team consisting solely of superstars. Look for a productive mix of people with bright ideas, people who are good starters and finishers, and people who can keep slogging away even when things look bleak.

■ *Look for a positive attitude.* You can nurture and develop someone who's a bit short of the skills that you need, if they're full of enthusiasm and committed to doing their best. However, someone who's cynical and obstructive will just be a drain on the project team whatever skills they possess. So, if you have to make a choice, favour attitude over skills.

■ *Don't think: anybody is better than nobody.* Don't be tempted to take on someone who isn't quite right for the job. Invariably a disproportionate amount of time is wasted trying to fit a square peg into a round hole. If in doubt say no.

■ *Remember the practical things that make a person effective.* Things like a desk, a chair, tools for the job, a security pass and computer user accounts. Sounds obvious, but time after time we've seen new team members turn up and find that no preparation has been made for their arrival.

But by far the most common recruiting mistake is panic buying of masses of extra resource to meet an impossible target. It's a fallacy that ramping up project resources late in the day is a solution to meeting a deadline that's in danger of being missed. This course of action tends to be counterproductive.

The time that's spent on securing and inducting a new resource is usually underestimated. The considerable drain on current team members as they bring the new people up-to-speed is also often overlooked. The net effect is that recruitment of additional resource can actually result in a reduced team capability for several weeks, as the new team members are found and absorbed. A project would usually be better off focusing its resource on completing the job at hand as efficiently as possible, rather than being distracted by an eleventh-hour recruitment drive.

It shouldn't happen to a project manager (but it did) . . .

A project was falling behind and resources were severely stretched. As deadlines approached, the project manager released two under-performing staff and things improved. Later on, another team member was let go and the project eventually went in on time and under budget.

Recruiting is not the only way to improve average performance.

Motivating your team

A friend of ours once conducted an unusual survey. Towards the end of an office social event, he asked: 'How near to your full capacity do you operate at?' For a number of reasons the responses he received were candid and a consistent picture emerged. Everyone was operating at well below their maximum capacity – all at between 40% and 70%. This was hardly a scientific assessment, but we believe this straw poll corresponds to what we've seen in the workplace.

On the positive side, this anecdotal evidence tells us that everyone has significant scope for working more productively if they're suitably *motivated*. In fact you may well have seen this effect on a project, with a fast-approaching deadline being the classic example. Suddenly the whole team seems to step up through several gears and all sorts of things that have been trundling along miraculously get finished. The trick is to achieve something near this level on a consistent basis, not just in response to a project crisis. As a brilliant project manager, you should make increased team productivity a primary target.

Conversely, everyone has the capacity to work even slower if they're *demotivated*. A manager can single-handedly scupper any chance of an improved work rate and this sometimes happens. It's an unfortunate fact of project life that motivating a team can require persistent and well-considered effort, but demotivation can be achieved in an instant.

Top five tips for demotivating

1   Be inconsistent for no apparent reason. Like being cheerful and easy-going one day, grumpy and vindictive the next.

2   Ask team members for their opinions on important decisions and then consistently ignore their advice.

3   When the team has to work extended hours to meet an important deadline, make sure you leave the office early.

4   When something goes well, take all of the credit for yourself. Even better, when something goes badly, find a culprit immediately.

5   Make promises you have no intention of keeping and then shrug them off as misunderstandings when delivery time comes.

Simple motivational techniques

It's easy to over-complicate motivational techniques and, like a yo-yo dieter, find yourself switching from one fad to another with only patchy results. We also believe that you should motivate people in an honest and open way, not as a devious attempt to manipulate them while they're looking the other way.

First, make sure that you avoid anything that *de*motivates. Put yourself in your team's position and ask yourself what you could do to undermine its morale. Then avoid doing these things like the plague! Once you've mastered *avoiding demotivation* it's time to ask yourself the following simple questions – even better, get feedback from your team.

■ *Have I set clear objectives for all of my team members?* Motivation is about being prepared to put effort into doing something specific. If team members are uncertain about what's expected, their productivity will plummet.

■ *Do the team members have a good understanding of what's going on in the project?* They're more likely to increase their contribution if they have some grasp of the bigger picture. This extends beyond simply being told the minimum your project manager thinks you need to know.

■ *Is the workload across the team consistent with its capacity and is it properly balanced?* If someone is overloaded they'll usually just give up or work themselves into the ground in a futile attempt to achieve the impossible. Both of these are a killer for motivation. So is having one part of the team sitting idle while others are working day and night.

■ *Are team members appropriately involved in decision making in the project?* If individuals feel that they can influence events they are far more likely to pull their weight. However junior you might be, there's nothing much worse than having your input consistently ignored.

Motivating individuals

While it's possible to motivate your team as a whole, project managers also recognise the importance of motivation at the individual level. This requires an understanding of what makes each individual in your team 'tick' and selecting the best motivational techniques to use.

With most people, a little investigation will soon begin to highlight what gets them going. You might find this out in general conversation, by observing them in action or simply through a bit of trial and error. Although motivation is a very individual thing, there are common motivators you'll come across in the workplace:

- *Sense of achievement.* Basking in the glory of having got something of importance done.

- *Seeing something completed.* Gaining satisfaction from having seen something through to the bitter end.

- *Enjoying a challenge.* Having the satisfaction of achieving something that you or others regard as difficult or demanding.

- *Career progression.* Undertaking something that furthers your longer-term career interests, even if the immediate task at hand is not that attractive in itself.

- *Peer pressure.* Feeling the need to meet the expectations of your colleagues.

- *Intellectual reward.* Enjoying the mental stimulation of a task that requires some thought or imagination.

Longer-term motivators

Some motivational techniques achieve a result that's immediate, but won't have lasting impact. For example, giving someone a pay rise can be a good short-term motivator, but rarely has a positive effect in the long term. People soon get used to a certain salary level and the bonus becomes a norm. Short-term techniques like this have an important place in the project manager's toolkit, but don't rely on them exclusively.

You'll need to develop long-term, sustained enthusiasm within the team and this is rarely achieved with one dramatic action. It requires the cumulative effect of numerous smaller measures, often seen as something-and-nothing in their own right, but with a greater joint impact. It's possible to refine the way in which you manage people and organise your project work so that almost everything you do has a positive motivational aspect.

Practical suggestions for building interest and enthusiasm

- *Set expectations.* Start with being clear about how you expect your team to behave and the standards you're looking for.

- *Set targets that are challenging yet achievable.* Set *some* objectives that are acknowledged as difficult to achieve and a 'stretch'. Most people respond to a challenge.

- *'Feel the heat.'* Arrange for team members to have a direct stake in important activities, rather than just a supporting role. For example, not just preparing the materials for a key presentation, but having a practical role in the event itself.

- *Find small but enjoyable rewards for staff.* For example, offering to pay for a meal out for a team member (plus partner) who's had to work extended hours.

- *Organise informal social events.* Something designed to create social interaction in a way that doesn't happen at work, such as an evening out bowling.

A project manager sets the tone for the project. If you have a gloomy outlook from the start your pessimism will be contagious and it will trigger a self-fulfilling prophecy. Contrast this with a brilliant project manager who believes the project is tough but doable if everyone pulls together as a team. So above all else, set an example by being enthusiastic and highly motivated yourself.

Providing leadership

So, you've built the right team and got them motivated. But do they know where they're going and how they're going to get there? More importantly, does the project manager know? If you don't have clear sight of the ultimate project goals and a firm idea of how to get there, it will be impossible for you to provide effective leadership. The end result will be a team that's either sitting idle or rushing off in different directions.

A solid plan is the foundation for effective leadership, but much more is required to inspire your team. A brilliant project manager needs to work in a way that creates confidence and brings out the best in individuals. You can learn and develop much of this behaviour and here are important areas for you to focus on:

- *Setting an example.* Through the way that you behave you should set standards that you want others to follow.

- *Never giving up.* You need to be prepared to stick at things until they're complete.

- *Being honest but tactful.* Honesty is the best policy, but don't pursue this in a way that undermines your working relationships.

- *Acting even-handedly.* Treat everyone equally and fairly, even if you have your favourites.

- *Being persuasive.* You need to get your facts straight, to put together a solid line of reasoning and to be convincing. Remember that the way you deliver your argument can be as important as the argument itself.

Dictatorship or democracy?

There are many different styles of leadership ranging from the auto-cratic to the consultative. It's essential for your leadership style to sit comfortably with your character traits. If you're an easy-going fan of consensus reaching then an aggressive management style will be unconvincing. Similarly, if you feel you must call the shots without much room for debate, a more consultative style of working is not for you.

However, brilliant project managers are able to adapt their management style to suit their projects. This involves being awake to the culture of the organisation you're working in, the nature of the project you have to deliver and the immediate project priorities. A valuable asset is being able to recognise the situations in which you need to adjust your leadership style.

While you need to be careful about generalisations where people matters are concerned, it's our view that a consultative approach is far more productive *most of the time*. People rise to the challenge better when they feel involved. However, there's a big difference between being consultative and running your project by committee.

A project manager needs to listen to the team, but ultimately makes the decisions. A brilliant one knows when to go against the popular view. Being totally driven by the team can be as counterproductive as not listening to it at all.

Hands-on or hands-free?

Another aspect of leadership style is the extent to which you are a 'hands-on' or 'hands-off' manager. Many project managers are promoted up through the ranks and have an almost uncontrollable urge to be hands-on – especially if they're true experts in the field. They believe it will be quicker to do the jobs themselves and they will be done better too.

It can be very hard for a new project manager to let go. Often they're right in the simplest sense about comparative abilities, but it's impossible to deliver anything apart from small, simple projects single-handedly. It's important to stop working on the project and to start managing it.

We're not arguing in favour of a totally hands-free approach and there are times when the team will appreciate your expert intervention. But do this too often and you'll run the risk of being seen as dabbling and interfering. A brilliant project manager is aware of the pros and cons and only intervenes judiciously.

Hands-on or hands-off?		
	Advantages	Disadvantages
Hands-on	■ Good first-hand knowledge of what's happening at ground level. ■ Can intervene directly and quickly.	■ Can undermine team members through persistent intervention. ■ Can be easily sidetracked away from project management responsibilities.
Hands-off	■ Team members are told what to do rather than how to do it. ■ Can concentrate on core project management tasks.	■ Can become out of touch with what's happening on the ground. ■ Can appear remote from team members.

You've got to get the balance right. You need to be sufficiently hands-off so that your team feels a strong sense of responsibility for delivery, but not to the extent that problems are allowed to get out of hand or you lose touch with your project.

Crisis? What crisis?

No matter how well a project is planned and managed, it's inevitable that something significant is going to go wrong at some point. Perhaps the neighbourhood's lights go out when one of your diggers severs a buried power cable. It's at times of crisis that a project manager's people skills are put to the test and any chickens thinking about a bed for the night finally decide to come home to roost.

Barker & Cole's world of simple definitions

A **project** is a unique piece of work, with a defined beginning and end. And at least one major crisis.

Crises show up how well a team is organised and motivated. They also provide a good test of leadership skills. With help from the team, a brilliant project manager will deal with each crisis and emerge with a stronger team and an enhanced personal reputation.

Where a dictatorial project manager is in command, at the first sniff of a crisis a witch-hunt will be launched and the culprit hunted down. This can create a temporary fear factor, where team members work harder to avoid a repetition. However, for someone trying to motivate their team and to achieve sustainable success, a crisis presents an excellent opportunity to build respect and goodwill: essential assets for a brilliant manager.

When it hits the fan, instead of looking for a culprit, concentrate on solving the problem. Don't ask 'Who's responsible?', ask: 'What needs to be done to fix the problem?' Don't look to offer up a sacrificial lamb to senior management, show leadership by demonstrating you're in charge and actively looking for a solution. In fact, in times of crisis it's especially important that you demonstrate that responsibility rests with you as project manager.

More often than not, relatively small problems are blown out of all proportion and on closer, considered inspection there's a solution or at least a way of working around the problem. So it's essential to remain calm and to concentrate on working out the way forward. Your handling of an alleged crisis will be *remembered* by your team.

Summary

People skills are as important to being a brilliant project manager as the ability to produce a sound project plan or to maintain a slick risks and issues log. That's because so much to do with project management involves dealing with people. One minute you'll be coaxing a reluctant team member to get on with the job, the next trying to placate a demanding customer; and all this while trying to juggle project responsibilities.

Forget the popular notion that it's only hard-nosed, take-no-prisoners project managers who get results. Many kinds of leadership styles are successful, and it's important that you work in a way you're comfortable with. However, there's much to be gained from taking a consultative approach – and this isn't the same thing as decision making by committee. An important part of project leadership is showing that you're ultimately responsible for everything that happens on your project, and this includes taking all the important decisions.

Don't ignore the obvious motivators and demotivators, and always remember that your team is made up of individual characters. What gets them up in the morning and what can you do to get the best out of their talents? You'll need to find the answers to these questions if your team's going to reach the levels of productivity that are possible – but not the norm.

It's amazing how word spreads when a project manager is good to work for and 'alright I suppose' (team members will never publicly admit to much more than this). This gives you an added extra: the kind of team members you'll want in your team will be keen to work for you.

Barker & Cole's final word on *leading effective teams* ...

- You're only as good as your team.

- When it comes to productivity, don't settle for the norm – you can do much better than that.

- One size doesn't fit all. Don't be afraid to experiment with motivational techniques until you find what works best.

- Don't steal glory and don't pass on blame.

- Remember there are times when nobody is better than any old body.

- If you don't know where your project's going, your team certainly won't!

Chapter seven

productive
meetings

running the best
get-togethers in town

> **"A meeting is an event where minutes are taken and hours are wasted."**
>
> Anon

Introduction

There's a prevailing image of the project manager as someone who calls endless, pointless meetings. To many, it appears as though project managers spend much of their time locking up their key personnel and taking everyone away from doing *real work*.

However, few people doubt the importance of the free flow of information in an organisation. Whenever we've conducted staff surveys, 'communication problems' are regularly at the top of the gripe list in some form or another. So you'd think that getting people together would be seen as a positive step. Clearly there's some sort of disconnection here; something's definitely going wrong.

Project managers use many ways to communicate. These include informal face-to-face conversations, email, direct phone calls, meetings and workshops. However, it's common to find that team members invariably reserve their most scornful wrath for the endless procession of meetings, meetings and more meetings that they're subjected to. It's a communication mechanism that's both heavily used and heavily criticised.

We very much agree with the popular complaints about meetings. However, we think they have a bad press. While we all have plenty of personal experience of meetings that were simply a waste of time, there's nothing fundamentally wrong with them. It's just that organisations typically don't do meetings very well. Most sessions are poorly prepared for, poorly executed and lack the right follow-up. This all conspires against any prospect of them being effective. This is a great shame because projects desperately need well-run meetings as part of their staple diet for success.

Barker & Cole's home truths

Too many meetings are like ceilidhs (*an informal social gathering at which there is Scottish or Irish folk music, singing, dancing and story telling*) without the music, singing and dancing.

Meetings will play an important part in any project you manage – for good or for bad. Some simple but effective measures can make all the difference between frittering away time for no particular gain and moving your project along at pace. Therefore, productive meetings are pivotal to brilliant project management and that's why we're dedicating a chapter solely to this much-maligned subject.

Meetings come in many flavours

Under the generic umbrella of meetings we include anything from an informal, ad-hoc meeting in the corridor through to a large-scale presentation – with all the standard project management type sessions in between. The core of any project meeting is its objective – its *raison d'être*. In a project environment a meeting typically serves one of three broad purposes (or a combination thereof):

- *To plan or review progress*. Planning, reviewing progress and replanning are at the heart of project management and can be done either one-on-one or as a team event. We prefer interactive group sessions for any significant planning work or major project reviews.

- *To make decisions*. Decisions are continually being made on projects and many of these require getting the right people together with the right information to arrive at an informed conclusion.

- *To do constructive work*. People regularly need to be brought together to work on deliverables. For example, to agree and prioritise requirements at the start of a project.

If a meeting does not have at least one of these broad objectives, the alarm bells should start ringing.

Barker & Cole's top tips

Be sparing in calling lengthy meetings involving large numbers of people. Ten people at a three-hour meeting equates to the best part of a working week!

Although there are many *flavours* of meetings – informal, formal, regular, irregular, planned, ad hoc, one-on-one, large scale – we recommend they all adhere to the same basic structure and disciplines:

- *preparation*: laying the foundations for a productive session;
- *execution*: running the meeting to achieve its objectives;
- *follow-up*: reaping the benefits of the meeting.

Let's look at each of these in turn.

It's all in the preparation

If you are a meeting *voyeur*, it becomes clear within a few minutes of the start of any get-together whether it's going to be productive or not. In fact the fate of the meeting is normally determined long before the meeting starts, because *it's all in the preparation*.

It never ceases to amaze us how little effort goes into preparing for meetings. Many meeting organisers decide to wing it and this is one of the most common reasons why meetings fail to serve a useful purpose. It's inexcusable to call a meeting without clear, specific objectives and a supporting agenda. Achieving the detailed objectives of a meeting is the measure of its success and the agenda provides the path for getting there.

Here are some simple steps for organising a meeting.

Organising meetings: it's as easy as 1–2–3

1   *Set objectives and an agenda.* Never organise a meeting without deciding what its purpose is. If you're not sure what you want, then you're not ready to meet.

   ■ Decide what you want to get out of the meeting. Ensure your objectives are specific and that they're achievable with the time and participants available.

   ■ Design an agenda that will achieve your meeting objectives. Don't forget to include items to introduce and to summarise the session. Be realistic about how long each agenda item will take.

   ■ Circulate the objectives and agenda in advance, and ask for comments on these beforehand. Ensure there's sufficient time for attendees to undertake any preparatory work that might be required.

2   *Get the right people to attend.* Clear objectives and an excellent agenda will be no use if the wrong people turn up.

   ■ Make sure the attendees you need are available.

   ■ Keep the number of attendees tight and consistent with the kind of meeting event being organised.

   ■ Make sure you and your attendees can cover the roles of chair, scribe and timekeeper.

3   *Pay attention to the physical arrangements.* Physical arrangements might seem trivial but can cause havoc if not sorted out properly.

   ■ Choose the right meeting location. Sometimes you'll want to make the location as convenient as possible. Other times you'll want to take people away from the distractions of their work environment.

- Ensure your meeting venue has the space and equipment you require. You may well need to bring along some things yourself. (Have you noticed that whiteboards always seem to be stocked with an impressive array of pens that don't work?)

- Set up the venue to reflect the kind of meeting you're organising. For example, if you want to have a round-table discussion, a room laid out in lecture theatre style will work against you.

Avoid delegates and no-shows

One of the most difficult aspects of preparing for a meeting involves getting the right people to attend. Your starting point must be to make sure not only that all the required individuals are invited but also that they show up without sending delegates in their place.

Delegates are one of the great plagues of modern meetings. You've invited all the right people, but a couple of gofers or lackeys turn up who are poor substitutes. It's a bit like your ideal partner sending a friend on your first proper date – it can be an improvement but rarely is.

Where there's any risk of delegates or no-shows, canvass the key attendees and ask them in person whether they're coming. If they waiver, use your personal skills to persuade them to attend. Having done the right preparation, you'll be able to explain to them why they specifically have been invited, what role you need them to play in the meeting and what the implications are if they're not able to attend.

Key roles and responsibilities

In preparing for a meeting you need to sort out the principal roles in advance. These are:

- *Chair.* Responsible for the overall running of the meeting. Take on this role yourself in all but exceptional circumstances.

- *Scribe.* Responsible for the meeting minutes. Assign this to a trusted meeting attendee.

- *Timekeeper*. Responsible for tracking progress against the agenda's planned timings. Ask for a volunteer to take on this job.

The chair orchestrates the meeting and must be effective because this is the most critical role. It's important to keep focused, but fair-minded and tolerant. This is a tricky balance to achieve and we'll be looking at the facilitation aspect in detail in the next chapter.

It's tempting to see the scribe role as a menial administrative function. However, it's usually a job that requires a fair degree of skill. The scribe needs to have a keen eye – or rather ear – for what merits recording. There's then the challenge of capturing the essence of decisions and actions while the meeting is in full flow. The scribe also needs to have the confidence to speak up to pause the meeting if clarification is required or something has been agreed that simply doesn't make sense.

For a small meeting it might be possible for the chair to take on the role of scribe. However, for anything more demanding you should be wary of trying to combine the roles. It's simply too difficult to take good-quality notes, while simultaneously controlling the dynamics of the meeting and sticking to the meeting agenda. Besides, by working as a double act, a chair and scribe can exert the required control over how the meeting is conducted.

Life is pretty straightforward for a timekeeper. They simply need a watch and to remember to keep an eye on it. They also need to be willing to speak out when a pre-agreed time is approaching. The timekeeper doesn't need to worry if a call time comes at an unfortunate point in the meeting. It's the chair's role, with input from the other attendees, to make a decision on how to deal with time pressures. The timekeeper can also be the chair's best friend, providing the perfect reason to close down a rambling discussion and to move on.

Consider hi-tech options

Technology offers some practical alternatives to meeting face-to-face, with most organisations having access to telephone or video-based conferencing facilities. These can certainly save considerable time and expense where meeting participants are scattered around the country or even around the world.

However, we've found that these kinds of sessions work best when the participants have already formed an effective working relationship. For initial meetings we recommend being there in person if at all possible. We've also found that conference calls are best interspersed with in-person ones, even when everyone's on first-name terms. Some useful business can be done in the margins of face-to-face meetings, with the opportunity of an additional social event where people have travelled and are staying over. There's also evidence that constant use of tele- and video-conferences can encourage an 'us and them' mentality that erodes team spirit.

Top tips for preparing a meeting

- *Make sure there's plenty of contingency for each agenda item.* Agenda items always take more time than you think, and besides, you're unlikely to get lynched for finishing a meeting a little early.

- *Punctuate your agenda with well-planned comfort breaks.* You're unlikely to keep a group productive for more than 1½ hours. Also remember you'll do well to contain a break to anything less than 15 minutes.

- *Don't invite more than seven other participants if you want to hold a truly interactive session.* Any more and people will be inhibited from contributing and the meeting will probably end up being dominated by one or two fearless talkers.

- *Don't avoid key players because they're troublesome or don't agree with you.* But avoid going into hostile territory alone or under-prepared.

- *A meeting room that's too hot or cold can single-handedly scupper your preparations.* Locate those heating controls or move the meeting somewhere else!

Orchestrating a successful meeting

You'll usually be acting in the role of chair and therefore be wielding significant influence over how each event unfolds. Even when the right preparation has been done, it's important the meeting gets off to a flying start. The opening is likely to set the tone for the meeting as a whole. Make sure you're the first one in the room, and greet everyone as they arrive – especially if it's likely to be a controversial or contentious meeting. The informal pre-meeting niceties need to be managed too!

Start proceedings off by welcoming everyone in a bright, positive way without going overboard. A smile and a friendly greeting can create a good atmosphere that will spill over into the meeting proper. It's also an opportunity to introduce yourself to anyone who doesn't know you.

Next, set the key meeting ground rules up-front. It's easy to alienate people if you come across like a scolding schoolteacher, so be careful to outline the meeting etiquette deftly. For example, there's no point in antagonising someone from the start just because their mobile is switched on. So, as you turn off your own mobile, make the observation, 'I always forget to turn this thing off!' You'll find that most reasonable people follow suit.

Top five ways to kill a meeting early on

1   Arrive ten minutes late.

2   Start off with a lengthy chitchat about your favourite hobby – sport is a popular option.

3   Raise doubts about the purpose of the meeting.

4   Announce you'll be leaving halfway through; preferably handing over to someone who is reluctant to take on this responsibility.

5   Start the meeting proper by immediately going off-piste and discussing an item that's not on the agenda.

Ultimately, developing the skills required to be an effective chair comes with practice, but it helps to stick to a few, very simple rules:

- Always open by summarising the purpose of the meeting and reviewing the agenda.

- Keep focused on the topics on the agenda.

- Keep close to the times agreed for each agenda item; and certainly start and end the event on time.

- Encourage active participation from *all* attendees.

- At the end of the session, summarise and confirm all the agreed decisions and actions.

Although the chair will set the pace and lead by example, it's very important to have other people in the meeting who are sympathetic and supportive. For example, if you need a controversial idea or decision to be discussed, it's more effective to have someone else in the meeting primed to raise the point. You'll then be able to influence the direction of the discussion, without simply being seen to dominate the meeting.

Barker & Cole's home truths

Domestique is French for 'servant' and is used as a cycling term for a team player who sacrifices individual performance to help the team. Every project manager needs a collaborator – to use another French expression – someone who arrives on time, keeps to the designated etiquette and completes their actions in a timely fashion.

Our final tip for the meeting chair is to make use of a meeting 'car park'. This is an area – usually on a flipchart or whiteboard – that can be used to park points raised during the meeting that are perfectly valid, but which fall outside of its scope. The car park is a useful device for enabling the meeting chair to keep the session on track, but without being seen to ignore contributions. However, for this to be effective, it's important that the car park is always visible and agreement is reached on how each parked item will be dealt with outside of the meeting.

It shouldn't happen to a project manager (but it did) …

A project manager started work on a huge programme for a telecoms company in Ireland. Programme meetings were held in a lavish boardroom setting and attended by all the key project managers involved – close to 30 at times. The project manager's boss impressed on him the importance of his first meeting appearance, and they spent time rehearsing his maiden update together. The project manager paid great attention to every detail imaginable in the run up to the meeting. Nothing was left to chance.

The day of the project manager's big moment arrived. As he approached the boardroom – ten minutes early at 09:50 – the businesslike tones from within sounded ominous. Like a bolt of lightning it hit him! The meeting started at 09:00 each week, not 10:00! He'd mixed up the start time with another weekly meeting and so missed his slot.

As the old saying goes: you never get a second chance to make a good first impression. Never take the simple stuff for granted!

Reap what you've sown

Many see the end of a meeting as job done, but it's rare for it to be a neatly self-contained event that doesn't have resulting actions. So in reality, the benefit of a meeting lies as much in what happens after it as during it. It's therefore imperative for you to ensure that decisions and actions are followed up.

The follow-up process actually begins in the meeting itself, with the scribe taking minutes. At this point, perhaps an image of a nitpicker taking meticulous notes springs to mind; someone producing a blow-by-blow account of a session you didn't want to sit through in the first place. Embedded in the text will be a couple of vague actions you can't remember agreeing to. It doesn't need to be like this. Minutes are your friend and provide important control documents for your project.

Only three types of entry are valid in minutes:

- *Decisions* – documenting any key agreements made. The entry needs to record only who made the decision and the decision itself.

- *Actions* – specifying any follow-up task assigned to *an individual at the meeting*. The entry needs to document the action, the individual who has overall responsibility for the task and the date by which it must be completed.

- *Supporting notes* – summarising any supporting information that is essential for providing the context for the recorded decisions and actions. To be used rarely, or at least sparingly.

Barker & Cole's top tips

Ensure each meeting action states precisely what needs to be done and the date it needs to be done by – and someone present at the meeting takes ownership. Vague action points are a recipe for confusion and inaction.

Where the minutes might be contentious, get them agreed during the meeting. It can be perceived as a bit tedious to review each key point – either as it's recorded or *en masse* at the end. However, this technique is great for confirming a shared understanding of what's been agreed and can save hours of work dealing with post-meeting disagreements.

We've found that prompt issue of minutes makes a big difference to the likelihood of the agreed actions being followed through. By prompt we mean ideally the same day, but no later than close of business the next working day. As we've already outlined, minutes don't need to be an onerous chore and putting off writing them up undermines the whole point. It also sends out the wrong message about your own commitment to action. Book time after the meeting with the scribe to get minutes issued while the discussion is fresh in your mind.

Having got the minutes out in a timely fashion, it's then essential that you track progress on the agreed actions and chase them up if required. You'll need an effective mechanism for doing this and an actions log sitting alongside your risks and issues log is a useful tool.

You'll soon find that active meeting follow-up creates a virtuous circle. Once people see that their meeting commitments are not going to be quietly forgotten, they're more likely to get on with whatever they agreed to. Next time around they'll also think that little bit harder about what they sign up to at one of your meetings.

Think big by thinking small

It's extremely easy to overlook, or underutilise, the power of small, semi-informal meetings. Think back on how much you achieved at less formal events; perhaps chance conversations in the corridor or the lift. People seem more relaxed, perhaps less on their guard, when the setting is informal.

We're not suggesting you adopt a *totally* Machiavellian approach to your chance encounters, but we do promote better use of seizing the moment or dropping in to see people. All we're recommending is a quick, automatic mental check of the business potential in these situations and a more systematic approach to exploiting the opportunity. As you can see, our basic meeting principles are scalable and can be used on anything from a large workshop to a one-to-one.

Barker & Cole's world of simple definitions

Where two or more people are gathered, anything more than a social chitchat is a **meeting**.

This approach is especially useful when you're dealing with senior management or anyone with a meeting phobia. Senior managers rarely have time for lengthy meetings, and you can chase your tail trying to pin down their availability. In our experience, it's far easier to wait for a chance encounter or to fashion one. Wait for the customary greeting of 'How's it going?' and hit them with what you want. We strongly advise having one request in mind, not a barrage – ask for too much and you'll get nothing. Look upon these meetings as coming across a reluctant genie – someone who can grant your dearest wish but isn't going to make the first move.

However, a word of warning: beware of falling into the trap that semi-informal meetings don't need the same kind of rigour as 'proper' meetings. You need to be suitably prepared if you're going to get a decision or some action agreed. Ask yourself what you're looking to achieve. What's your precise objective for this encounter and what's the best tack to take? If you're not prepared, your ad hoc meeting may well prove to be a backward step.

Also, always make sure that anything of significance is documented at the next available opportunity. Often a friendly follow-up email that captures the important points you discussed will suffice. If these discussions are not recorded they can become counterproductive; you may well become a victim of conflicting memories and at the mercy of hearsay.

Barker & Cole's top tips

Review recurring meetings periodically and check whether they're still really necessary. Don't fall into the trap of holding regular 'project meetings' without good reason.

Summary

Have you ever heard anyone say: 'The agenda was clear, the right people attended and we started on time. The chair was focused and everyone contributed. How did it all go wrong?' The discipline needed to run successful meetings isn't hard to master but it can be difficult to apply consistently.

Meetings are going to play a major part in your project and for you to be a brilliant project manager it's important they're highly productive. The foundation for success lies in the preparation. Ensure you arrive at your well-chosen meeting venue with a solid agenda and the right people in attendance. Make sure that your meeting roles are sorted out in advance of the event.

Once the meeting is under way be alert to how effectively your chair, scribe and timekeeper are doing their jobs – even if that's you wearing three different hats! Make sure you stick to the agenda and that all important actions and decisions are recorded. Don't overrun. Build up a reputation as someone who runs a tight ship, not someone who shoots from the hip.

Meetings are not only an important part of brilliant project management, they're your showcase as a project manager. Many people will only see you in action during these sessions. If your meetings are tight and focused, not only will you get what you need out of them, your reputation as a project manager will be justly enhanced too.

Barker & Cole's final word on *productive meetings* . . .

- Always put the time needed into meeting preparation – it's the only way of ensuring that your meetings will be effective.

- No meeting should go ahead without an agenda, supported by a statement of its purpose and objectives.

- By default, take the role of the chair at meetings and make sure you have the right people acting as scribe and timekeeper.

- Meeting follow-up starts with the production of a set of punchy, action-oriented minutes. Get these issued without delay.

- Have a system in place to ensure you always follow up on meeting action points.

- Above all, create a virtuous circle for your meetings. Get a reputation as a brilliant project manager who runs the best get-togethers in town.

facilitation
skills

the show must go on

> **"** Gettin' good players is easy. Gettin' 'em to play together is the hard part. **"**

Casey Stengel (1890–1975)

Introduction

It's said that 'two heads are better than one' and most would agree that it's easier to develop a new idea or to solve a difficult problem when you've got someone to work with. On a similar theme 'a problem shared is a problem halved' and 'many hands make light work'. These popular adages illustrate the great potential of teamwork. If channelled effectively, groups of people can pool their collective knowledge and experience to impressive effect.

To tap into the immense potential of teamwork you'll need to be a *facilitator* and an *enabler*. By this, we mean someone who uses their people skills to make it easy for your colleagues to achieve their maximum contribution – both individually and as part of your team.

You need to get collective, collaborative working happening in all kinds of ways. This will range from everyday events like one colleague bouncing an idea off another, through to larger-scale, set-piece events such as project meetings and workshops. Whichever way, a brilliant project manager smoothes the path and makes it all possible. So although facilitation isn't traditionally found in the job description, we see it as one of the core competencies for brilliant project management.

Facilitation is a discipline in its own right, with its own specialist set of tools and techniques. Although it's not necessary to become an expert in the field, it's essential you're capable of facilitating project meetings and workshops. In this instance, your capabilities will make all the difference.

As with the other people skills we've covered, *facilitation* is a well-documented subject and your competency will grow with practice, experience and further research. Our aim here is to review the fundamentals of facilitation from a project perspective and to run through the practical techniques that we think every project manager should master.

Project managers as facilitators

Some people earn their living working exclusively as facilitators. Typically they're independent of projects – often brought in from outside the organisation – dipping in and out when needed. They tend to be used to lead important workshops and high-profile meetings.

However, in our experience, relatively few organisations employ their own full-time facilitators and only a small number bring in independent specialists on an occasional, as-needed basis. In fact, the vast majority of organisations don't use recognised facilitators at all. You might be lucky enough to have a specialist like this to run some of your key events. More often than not, though, you'll be expected to do this job at the same time as contributing to the discussion in some useful way.

We don't see this as a problem. Although the Facilitators' Union will see our comments as close to outright heresy, we usually prefer to handle our own facilitation. A brilliant project manager is quite capable of facilitating and has the added advantage of a first-hand understanding of what's good for the project in the widest sense. It's the best of both worlds and the organisational logistics are much simpler too!

It shouldn't happen to a project manager (but it did) . . .

A senior project manager was asked to deliver a session on the 'Fundamentals of Facilitation' as part of an internal training programme. Two junior project managers were drafted in to help deliver the material – as *training-within-training*. Despite their nerves, the two newcomers got the presentation off to a flying start. They were just about to hand over to their senior colleague when a mobile phone rang. They watched in amazement as their mentor disappeared out of the room to take the call.

Experienced managers aren't necessarily brilliant facilitators. If you don't have a natural aptitude, you'll need to put effort into developing your skills.

As we've said, though, there's much more to facilitation than running meetings. In fact, there's a touch of facilitation in everything you do as a project manager. For example, there are elements of *facilitation* in sorting out a dispute between two team members, just as there's a good measure of *enabling* in building an effective team. However, there are three everyday project situations in which your facilitation skills will be vital:

1 *When new ideas need to be generated.* For example, when customer requirements need to be captured at the start of a project.

2 *When a problem needs to be solved.* For example, when the team has produced a flawed product and you need to work out what's gone wrong and how it can be fixed.

3 *When you need to get people with different views to reach agreement.* For example, when you're faced with a number of possible designs for your project and each has its enthusiastic supporters and vociferous detractors.

In the remainder of this chapter we're going to explore the principles behind facilitation and then pick out some practical techniques that can be used in these common project situations.

Key principles behind successful facilitation

You'll need to use your facilitation skills in all kinds of situations and fortunately there are some basic underlying principles that will always point you in the right direction. In any given circumstance, we recommend you set yourself four fundamental goals, each of which is critical to successful facilitation and deserves a closer look.

Four fundamental facilitation goals

1 *To provide a process.* To provide an appropriate and reliable method for working through the problem or decision in question.

2 *To get people working collaboratively.* To get the right people together and to get them in the right frame of mind to work together productively.

3 *To introduce a degree of challenge.* To ensure opinions, conclusions and decisions are given the right level of scrutiny before they're accepted.

4 *To have some initial ideas.* To kick-start the process when there's a shortage of inspiration, or when things start to stutter and stall.

Providing a process

The starting point for facilitation is to provide a suitable method for working on a particular problem or issue. By taking responsibility for defining the mechanics of *how* a piece of work is going to be done, you'll enable your attendees to focus their attention on the specifics of *what* needs to get done. You'll also put yourself in a good position to steer your colleagues towards an end result that's fit-for-purpose.

On the flip side, the consequences of *not* providing a process are likely to be costly. Valuable time will be lost debating how the work should be tackled and the friction caused among the participants might result in an immediate setback to a successful outcome. Even worse, the team may try to tackle the task in a hit-and-miss fashion, disappearing off on tangents and stumbling into dead ends.

The process you introduce will provide a series of logical steps for resolving a problem or making a decision. It will be tailored to your project situation and may be influenced by relevant standards – or simply best practice in your particular field or industry. Above all else, it must be simple to understand and easy to use.

There are some straightforward questions you can ask yourself, to help check you've picked the right process.

- *Is the process well suited to dealing with the problem or issue? Is it fit-for-purpose?* Make sure your approach is tailored to achieving your precise objectives. Run through the steps with a colleague to test it out.

- *Is the approach practical considering both the number of people and the specific individuals involved?* Think carefully if you are dealing with a very large group or with born troublemakers.

- *Is it necessary to assign specific, individual responsibilities to the participants?* You need to be confident of their cooperation, so at least sound them out beforehand.

▶

> ■ *Is there any risk that things won't run as smoothly as planned?* Make sure you've got a Plan B just in case you go down like a lead balloon.
>
> ■ *Is the process simple to understand and easy to use?* There's no point in picking a technique that requires completing a specialist degree course!

The answers to these questions will help you to refine your approach – or perhaps change it altogether if you begin to have doubts about the likely success of the process you have in mind.

Getting people working collaboratively

Once you've decided *how* you'd like people to work, the next step is to think about what you can do to ensure your team collaborates in a constructive way. The key to this usually lies in getting everyone actively involved and working together from the outset. It's important to establish an immediate rapport or you'll be facing a long uphill struggle.

It's impossible to provide a formula for getting a facilitated session off to a great start, since the number of variables involved makes each one unique. However, there are some practical measures worth considering that can improve your chances of leading a productive session.

Improving your chances of a productive session

■ *Get the right type of people involved.* You'll need the participation of people with the right skills and experience. You'll also need to think about the personalities involved. Enthusiasm, good communication skills and an open mind can be as important as good ideas.

■ *Choose the right facilitation techniques.* Select techniques that suit your material and the participants. For example, if you're dealing with a contentious issue, take some of the heat out of the situation by using a technique that gets people thinking in a factual and logical way.

- *Get everyone relaxed and interested from the start.* A well-chosen icebreaker is an excellent way to get people comfortable and interacting straight away. Get people talking, thinking and laughing.

- *Encourage everyone to contribute from the beginning.* Look out for people who don't want to take part or feel concerned about doing so. Find ways of demonstrating that you're interested in everyone's views. Reassure those who feel uncomfortable about speaking up; establish there's no such thing as a 'dumb question'.

As a final thought on getting people working well together, never underestimate the power of fun! You should always look for ways of making your facilitated sessions interesting, perhaps even entertaining at times but without appearing frivolous. You'll know from personal experience what a difference it makes to work on something that's captured your interest. This is particularly true where creative processes are concerned. After all, it's pretty difficult to come up with an inspirational idea when you're trying to stifle a yawn.

Introducing a degree of challenge

Once people get working together and build up a head of steam, it can be easy for them to get *too focused* and to develop tunnel vision. They become blinded to other possibilities and options, especially if some strong personalities begin to dominate. So a brilliant project manager needs to be prepared to counterbalance this by introducing a degree of challenge from time to time.

It's important for you to use your facilitation role to make sure that ideas and proposed decisions stand up to scrutiny, *before* they're finalised. You'll need to do this in a constructive way to maintain the goodwill of the participants, but once they see that you're helping them to improve the quality of their ideas, they'll be inclined to cooperate.

Typically, a few, well-chosen, open questions will get your colleagues thinking that bit harder. You can encourage them to look at a problem or decision from different perspectives. Suggest time is spent looking at the drawbacks to a preferred option, as well as its positive points. Think about alternative solutions, however good your first idea seems. Keep pressing for the team to take a fresh viewpoint.

By introducing a degree of challenge in your facilitation you'll be testing the resilience of the ideas put forward. It's far better to prod and probe when you can easily fix any shortcomings.

Barker & Cole's home truths

When someone says, 'Just to play devil's advocate for a minute...' it usually means that they don't agree with what's being said but don't feel they can say so outright.

Providing some initial ideas

Most of the time, facilitation is about managing the process and letting the participants do the hard work. However, there are some situations where you should roll up your sleeves and contribute directly to the discussion itself. For example:

- if the discussion needs to be kickstarted or is complex and needs initial channelling;

- when the creative process is getting bogged down or is in danger of going off-piste.

Sometimes you'll need to prepare material that can be used to spark discussion. This is because people usually find it easier to work from an initial idea than from scratch – even if that idea turns out to be not that great. It's important that you introduce this preparatory work as a starting point for discussion and not as a done deal. That way, you'll maintain the motivation of your contributors – which might waiver if they sense they've been presented with a *fait accompli*.

It's not always possible to prepare material ahead of time. For these occasions, or where a stalemate is developing, here are a few, easy-to-use techniques worth having up your sleeve:

- *Introduce a new angle.* Reinvigorate the discussion by getting people thinking about things from another perspective.

- *Change the subject, start on a new topic.* Car park the current discussion and come back to it later if necessary when minds are refreshed. A change is as good as a rest.

- *Take a break.* At times, all it takes is a ten-minute break to recharge everyone's batteries. A creative process can be intense and your team will need regular refuelling stops.

- *And don't flog a dead horse.* Recognise the law of diminishing returns.

Facilitation techniques for all occasions

As well as there being some useful guiding principles behind facilitation, there are plenty of practical techniques available to project managers. Whatever you're looking to achieve, you can be sure that there are some handy tools out there that will make your life easier. You don't even need to be a paid-up member of the Facilitators' Union to use them!

There are three facilitation techniques that we use most frequently. We like them because they're both simple and effective. They're also good, general-purpose tools.

Top three facilitation techniques for project managers

- *Brainstorming* – a popular technique used to generate numerous ideas using the combined talent and experience of a group in a facilitated meeting environment.

▶

■ *Criteria-based decision making* – a way of reaching a joint decision in a group when there are multiple options available.

■ *Root-cause analysis* – a technique for uncovering the underlying reason why something happened.

These techniques can be used in the three common project situations we highlighted earlier on: generating ideas, solving problems and reaching agreement. We'll outline how each technique can be used in these scenarios. However, you'll soon see that they're more widely applicable and can easily be combined in all sorts of useful ways.

Generating ideas

The creator of the brainstorming technique, advertising executive Alex Osborne, is famously quoted as saying: 'It is easier to tone down a wild idea than to think up a new one.' Brainstorming is based on this principle.

The aim of brainstorming is to generate lots of ideas to work from – with the emphasis initially on quantity rather than quality. Brainstorming is designed to get everyone in a group contributing. It also encourages participants to build on each other's ideas.

Brainstorming is a great technique to use when you need a comprehensive set of ideas in a relatively short space of time. It also has the advantage of working well with both small and large groups of people.

Simple guide to brainstorming

1 Clearly define the problem or opportunity to be worked on. For example: 'How can we shave 20% off our house-building budget?'

2 Ask participants to voice their ideas. All ideas are welcomed – even those that seem outlandish.

3   Record every idea. No discussion or evaluation of ideas is allowed, and nothing is ruled out.

4   Encourage people to build on the ideas of others.

5   Continue until you run out of steam.

Brainstorming is, without doubt, the most widely used and *mis*used facilitation technique. The most common mistake is to allow discussion and evaluation of ideas as they are recorded. This interrupts the free flow of ideas. Part of the success of brainstorming comes from people building on previous ideas, often by free association. So it's essential to emphasise the 'no discussion' rule at the beginning of any brainstorming session and then to enforce it throughout.

We're keen on one useful variation on the conventional brainstorming technique. Sometimes we ask participants to record all of their ideas on sticky notes. When everyone has finished, these are then stuck on a wall and common ideas grouped together. This approach cuts out any opportunity for debating ideas before they are recorded and also stops the whole group following just one line of thinking.

It's worth remembering that brainstorming is about *generating* ideas. It doesn't help with analysing the ideas once they're recorded. So you'll usually want to follow up a brainstorming session with a technique that organises and evaluates the ideas you've collected.

Consensus building

It can be difficult and time consuming to get individuals to make decisions when a number of competing factors need to be taken into account. This is especially true where the pros and cons are finely balanced, or people have taken entrenched positions and feelings are running high.

Even a brilliant project manager will regularly come across these situations during projects. In fact, you'd be right to start worrying if your team was in total agreement all of the time! Generally, healthy debate leads to an agreed decision. However, there are times when things are going nowhere fast and it's time to introduce an objective and systematic approach to decision making. It's also important to do this in a way that leads your participants towards some kind of group consensus. Our favourite by far is the *criteria-based decision making technique*. It's quite a mouthful, yet very effective and easy to apply.

Simple guide to criteria-based decision making

1   Define the decision that needs to be made. For example, 'What type of heating system should be installed in our new house?'

2   Identify and describe all the available options.

3   Agree the best criteria for comparing the options and then agree the relative importance of the assessment criteria – known as *weighting*. For example, running cost is three times as important as the lead-time on delivery.

4   Define a *simple* numerical scoring range for each criterion. For example: 1 to 10, where 1 is poor, 5 is average and 10 is excellent.

5   Get the participants to score each criterion within each option. Make sure that they are consistent in the way in which they award scores.

6   For each criterion, multiply the group's score by the weighting. Add up all the weighted scores to calculate each option's total score.

7   Rank the options according to final score and use the order as a basis for reaching agreement on the preferred option(s).

This technique's big selling point is that it breaks up decision making into simple, logical steps. The participants aren't able to argue in vague or emotive terms about what's right or wrong. Reasonable debate can only be had on whether the criteria being used need some refinement or whether the scores need adjusting. There's nothing wrong with this fine-tuning – even after the initial scoring – as long as it's not used to fix the outcome!

Criteria-based decision making also builds consensus step-by-step. First, it gets the participants to agree on what factors really matter most in making the decision. This is an important step in its own right. Then the technique requires agreement on each individual score. So by the time the final result emerges after the last step, no one is in a position to dismiss an option that's scored well or to urge the group to go for something that's languishing at the bottom of the list.

Barker & Cole's top tips

When consensus building, don't automatically select whatever scores best without further debate. Review the results of the exercise and discuss what lies behind the scores before making a final decision.

Solving problems

There are only three certainties in life: death, taxes and problems on projects. Your project will be peppered with dilemmas, but the biggest problem with problems is that it's easy to jump to hasty conclusions. You end up trying to fix what looks like the real issue, but which later turns out to be little more than a sideshow; worrying about a small wet patch on the bedroom ceiling when there's a gaping hole in the roof.

Root-cause analysis is a really effective way of getting to the heart of a problem. It helps you to separate out root causes from symptoms. This is important for long-term success, as a brilliant project manager wants to deal with underlying issues and not just to implement quick, short-term fixes. You can make root-cause analysis as complicated as you like, but we favour use of a simple approach based on asking the question: 'why?'

Simple guide to root-cause analysis

1   Produce a statement that defines the problem you want to work on. For example, 'paper is peeling off the ceiling in the master bedroom'. Write it at the top of a flipchart or whiteboard.

▶

2   Ask your participants *why* this problem has occurred. Encourage them to focus on the immediate causes.

3   Write their answers in a line across the flipchart or whiteboard, underneath your original problem statement.

4   Now take each new statement in turn and ask them 'why?'

5   Add the responses under the corresponding statement.

6   Repeat the process.

7   Stop when you start finding that causes are largely repetitive or they're things you have to accept as a fact of life. For example, 'because the house is a hundred years old'.

8   Get the participants to review the underlying root causes and to agree which should be targeted as project priorities.

For this technique to be successful, it's critical that you start with a problem statement that describes exactly the right issue. Your problem statement should be kept factual, objective and without any hint of underlying causes.

We've found that this technique consistently highlights what lies at the root of a problem. Then it's up to you and your team to decide on the most appropriate, cost-effective way forward. More often than not the solution lies in dealing with the root cause. However, a note of caution here: there are times when dealing with the root cause costs far more than dealing with the symptom. So you'll need to be pragmatic about the level at which you tackle a problem. Perhaps you could replace a few missing tiles on the roof rather than lay a completely new one!

Complementing techniques

The three techniques we've described provide you with an excellent grounding for dealing with most common project situations. Two of the reasons we like them so much is because they complement each other and they're also very easy to combine.

There'll be times *when new ideas need to be generated* but people have different opinions on which are best, and so *you'll need to get people with different views to reach agreement*. On other occasions, *when a problem needs to be solved* and you've identified the root cause, you might be stumped for a solution. You might view this as a situation *when new ideas need to be generated*.

Combining facilitation techniques: an example

Imagine that our house-building project has discovered a massive cost overrun and this looks set to get worse. Your construction team needs to get to the bottom of what's gone wrong and find ways of rectifying the problem.

You kick things off with a *root-cause analysis* to identify the factors that have contributed to the miscalculation. Having understood the underlying causes, you then run a *brainstorming* session to come up with ideas on how to turn the situation around. Once you've identified the most promising suggestions and developed them a little more, you use *criteria-based decision making* to pinpoint the top two or three ideas for a final team assessment. This combination of techniques is not the only way to reach agreement but it's structured, disciplined and highly likely to produce the right outcome.

After a while, you'll be surprised at how often you use all these facilitation techniques together – sometimes instinctively without even thinking. Once you feel confident with using our favourite techniques, you'll find it straightforward to master others.

Summary

Facilitation is all about helping your project to be creative when it needs to, to come to decisions when it should do and to remove roadblocks when it gets stuck. This gets to the very heart of brilliant project management as facilitation skills are essential for the day-to-day running of your project. They're also invaluable when tensions develop and you need to get people working collaboratively again.

For any situation there are some golden rules to stick to. First, take the lead in getting the right people together and provide them with a suitable process to work through. Then make sure that everyone contributes, not just those with the loudest voices. Once your team is beavering away, help it to reach the correct conclusions and to make sound decisions. Always be prepared to provide a bit of inspiration where this is in short supply and to give your team a head start where you can.

If you've mastered *brainstorming, root-cause analysis* and *criteria-based decision making*, you'll always have practical facilitation tools to use in any project situation. Be imaginative in combining and adapting these, and supplementing them with other techniques you find work for you.

Facilitation skills give you the means to get the most out of collaborative working. They also arm you with techniques for dealing with difficult people situations. So even if facilitation doesn't feature in your formal job description, work hard to make it one of your core skills.

Barker & Cole's final word on *facilitation skills* ...

- You're halfway to success once you've provided a process that's spot on.

- Don't leave home without your tool bag of simple and effective facilitation techniques.

- It's not a crime to make working together fun and interesting! Start your sessions with an icebreaker or something suitably invigorating.

- Go in search of opportunities to practise your facilitation skills. There's no substitute for hands-on experience.

- A brilliant project manager is a brilliant facilitator.

Chapter nine

making use

of lessons learned

brilliant mistakes

> **"You must learn from the mistakes of others. You can't possibly live long enough to make them all yourself."**
>
> Sam Levenson (1911–1980)

Introduction

The best way of avoiding mistakes is to do very little at all. Or you could stick religiously to the tried and tested, and avoid risk that way. However, neither option is a realistic one for a project manager – although over the years we've known a couple of people who have given it their best shot!

If you want your project to be productive and creative it's inevitable that mistakes will be made. Once you accept this, you'll see that managing a project is not about avoiding mistakes at all costs, it's about learning from them and not repeating them. A brilliant project manager goes one step further and also searches out lessons that *others* have learned.

It's worth reminding ourselves that what's gone well provides lessons too. This involves identifying good practice, and wherever possible promoting and repeating it. This is illustrated by the way a brilliant project manager will come armed with a range of good ideas and techniques from previous projects. This is equally a part of the *lessons learned* process, even if it's not always recognised as such.

Unfortunately the results of many lessons learned reviews end up sitting in a virtual electronic cupboard attracting cyber-dust. This is a waste of the time and effort spent on gathering lessons – not forgetting the cost of making the mistakes in the first place. So, although identifying lessons is an important step, the value lies in exploiting what you've learned. You'll see a return on your investment only when mistakes are avoided and good practice is repeated.

In this chapter we'll look at when and how you should set about capturing your project's lessons. We'll also look at the all-important step of putting these lessons to practical use.

How to make a pig's ear out of lessons learned

- Concentrate on mistakes. Name and shame the culprits.

- Put everyone in the firing line. Previous good work on the project is not a *get out of jail card* when someone makes a blunder.

- Specify exactly what went wrong in excruciating detail. Avoid drawing any wider conclusions.

- The more, the merrier! There is no substitute for volume and nothing is too trivial to mention.

- Use lessons learned to settle long-standing personal vendettas and grudges.

- Fire out your lessons learned report to all and sundry, especially to the bosses of your biggest enemies.

Have realistic expectations

In our experience, organisations aren't good at learning lessons. We see the same mistakes being repeated from one project to the next. We also see missed opportunities to replicate and build on good practice. There seems to be a lack of appetite – almost reluctance – to learn from past experience.

In many places, actively looking for things that could be done better or successes that should be repeated is not seen as a priority. In fact, time invested this way is seen as non-productive gilding of the lily. The emphasis is very much on just getting the immediate job done.

Some organisations *do* encourage the capture of lessons. However, too many then fail to take the important next steps of spreading the message and reapplying the experience gained. Sometimes this is because people believe their own circumstances are so unique that lessons learned 'over there' don't really apply to them 'over here'. At other times it's just a lack of appreciation of the potential goldmine on their doorstep.

Whatever the prevailing culture, a brilliant project manager knows lessons learned are always well worth pursuing. There's a great deal to learn from both your own and others' projects. Much can be applied with immediate effect or at the very least stored up for use on the next project that comes along.

Brilliant project managers are simply realistic. They know they can't change the world, but they *can* tap into a wealth of experience to make significant improvements to the way they run their projects.

It shouldn't happen to a project manager (but it did) . . .

An organisation set up an ambitious programme and got its initial set of projects up and running. The project managers who set off first soon realised that their colleagues following behind were heading for many problems they'd already solved. They decided to share their experiences and invited the others to a lessons learned presentation. None of their colleagues turned up. Apparently, they were 'too busy' trying to deliver their projects. The second half of the programme then repeated many of the mistakes that their peers had already cracked.

It can be very frustrating when others refuse to take advantage of the experience you've gained. But, as long as you've done everything you reasonably can, that's life.

All is not always lost for the greater good, as there are occasions when your lessons rub off on others. Sometimes because you've decided it's important enough to make the extra effort and sometimes just because you get lucky. However, don't hold your breath waiting for this to happen and see it as a nice little bonus when it does.

Creating a learning environment

The starting point for lessons to be learned is to create a project environment where it's acceptable to make mistakes – with everyone willing to own up and to help get things back on track without too much fuss. The same principle applies to things that go well. You want any tips or tricks to be shared around, not jealously guarded. An honest and open culture, built on trust and mutual respect, is an essential ingredient for getting the best out of your team anyway.

Getting this aspect of the project culture right is doubly important. If people don't feel they're able to speak up, you'll find out very late in the day that something has gone wrong. By then mistakes will be much more expensive to put right and more likely to blow your project plan out of the water. Even worse, your team could put effort into covering its tracks and hiding mistakes – time that should be used far more productively rectifying what's gone wrong.

It's also important that everyone involved in the project is encouraged to contribute to lessons, not just key personnel. For example, people on the periphery – or so-called bit-part players – can often offer useful insights that those close to the action might miss. In any event, you'll always find that each person has a different personal perspective on what's happened and what should be learned. So to develop a rounded picture you'll need a good cross-section of feedback. It's usually a good idea to extend an invite to your customers and suppliers too.

How to promote a learning culture

- *Lead by example.* Always be open about your own mistakes and highlight what the experience has taught you.

- *Encourage honesty and openness.* Respond constructively when team members tell you about their mistakes. In the first instance, concentrate on putting things right. Learn the lessons afterwards and don't badmouth the 'culprits'.

- *Never miss an opportunity to emphasise your philosophy.* Explain that making a mistake is not the end of the world and that the important thing is to learn something as a result.

- *Promote the positive side of lessons learned.* Identify the practical things that can be done to stop the same things going wrong in the future. Don't forget to look for successes that should be repeated.

- *Make sure that you have plenty of informal contact with your team members.* Some of your best insights will come from corridor conversations.

- *Never use a lessons learned exercise for pinning blame on individuals.* Lessons should never be a front for settling vendettas.

When's the best time to learn lessons?

On the rare occasions when a project team puts effort into capturing lessons, it's usually the last act before the project is formally closed down. It would be just a little unfair to say this is closing the gate after the project team has bolted, but it goes some way to explaining why many potentially useful reports end up forgotten.

A brilliant project manager doesn't wait until the end of the project to take stock. You should be alert to opportunities for learning lessons at all stages. This way, you give yourself the opportunity to make immediate adjustments to the way your project is run. It can also help you to fine tune on your own terms, rather than be forced into a major change in direction in response to a mounting crisis.

We know that in the real world you'll have a lot on your plate and this can make it difficult to be receptive to lessons learned. If nothing else, be prepared to take a closer look when events follow a familiar pattern – usually for the worse. Perhaps one of your suppliers consistently delivers a few days late or your meeting attendees keep cancelling at the last minute. Each event in itself might not be a major cause for concern, but taken as a whole there could be some deep-rooted, underlying causes that need teasing out and resolving for your immediate benefit.

Some of the best times to pick up lessons is when you see things go spectacularly wrong or extremely well. You'll be repaid in spades if the lesson is immediately reusable, and if not, at the least it will be captured for future use.

Barker & Cole's top tips

Don't leave gathering lessons learned to the end of your project. Start a lessons learned log on day one.

Although we've stressed the importance of learning lessons as you go, it's also good practice to factor in set, formal review points.

Recommended review points

1 *When starting a new project.* Review what you've learned from previous projects and collect lessons from your team. Plan how and when all the collated advice will be applied on the new project.

2 *When starting a new project stage.* Review what's been learned from recent project progress. Decide how your plan needs to be refined to take advantage of this experience.

3 *Just before project closure.* Consider what you've learned personally and collect lessons from your team. It may be too late for the current project, but your future projects will reap the benefit.

Not only will these reviews provide you with useful checkpoints and prompts, they'll also set the tone for your project. Your team will see this is something you value and take seriously.

Finally, don't just think about lessons to be learned when you have a bit of spare time available. When things are going wrong and you're under pressure, it's natural to want to put lessons learned to the bottom of your to-do list. However, this is probably the most important time for you to take the time to step back and think about what you need to be doing differently.

Barker & Cole's home truths

The *traditional* gathering of lessons at the end of the project bears no immediate fruit, but it will provide invaluable lessons to take on to your next project. The process is a long-term investment and should be viewed as such.

The art of capturing lessons

Even if you've fashioned an open culture and lessons are obvious to your team members, it doesn't follow that you'll automatically get to hear about them. Your team will be concentrating on its immediate delivery objectives. It's up to you to tap into your team's collective experience and knowledge, and to make sure that lessons are captured.

One of your most important other goals is to get to the *real* lessons to be learned. Don't simply take events at face value. Project situations are rarely as simple and clear cut as they seem, even where there's a fair degree of consensus within the team that black is white and white is black.

Most of your contributors will have only partial information about what's happened. You'll no doubt also come across a variety of opinions spanning superficial symptoms to important root causes. Most difficult of all, many will have already taken a parochial perspective on what lessons should be drawn – with the default position being that someone else is to blame.

The art of capturing lessons lies in getting a balanced view on what happened and then identifying the fundamental underlying opportunities for improvement.

Basic principles for capturing lessons

There are many ways you can go about capturing lessons, ranging from formal workshops through to informal corridor conversations. There's a common thread running through all of these events: people teasing out reusable lessons by drawing on their key experiences – both good and bad. Therefore, the same basic process applies.

How to capture lessons learned

1 *Select the participants.* Work out who's best placed to draw out the lessons learned. Make sure that you get a balanced cross-section and they have an open mind.

2 *Confirm the audience.* Be clear about who the lessons are aimed at. If they're going beyond the team, consider how this will influence the kinds of lessons you want to capture and the way in which they'll be described.

3 *Identify successes and failures.* Undertake an objective review of what went well and what could be done better next time.

4 *Develop the lessons to be learned.* Investigate the underlying reasons why events took the course they did. Agree what you'd do again and what you would do differently with the benefit of 20–20 hindsight.

5 *Document and review the lessons learned.* Summarise and write up what you've learned. Make sure that the people who contributed agree you've described things accurately.

Defining lessons can be an emotive process. It's difficult to make much progress if your participants let their personal feelings take over or they're reluctant to move beyond initial impressions. In particular, you need to overcome a natural tendency to look for nice, simple answers that conform to preconceived ideas. A well-known example of this is that all of the project's woes are down to having an incompetent project manager. Perish the thought!

Therefore, whether you're running a formal lessons workshop or just meeting informally with a couple of colleagues, it's essential that you use a logical and objective lessons learned process. You'll find that the facilitation techniques we covered in Chapter 8 are invaluable here. *Brainstorming* can be used to generate starting lists of what went well and what didn't. The important job of then separating out the key underlying issues from the surface-level symptoms can be achieved using *root-cause analysis*. Finally, *criteria-based decision making* can be a handy tool for whittling down the lessons to those that matter most. This kind of approach will get everyone working together objectively towards a result that the team thinks is a fair reflection of what should be learned.

Informal techniques for capturing lessons

Lessons learned sessions don't have to be big set-piece meetings that require vast amounts of time and effort to organise. Informal techniques can pay big dividends and, at times, are far more successful at getting to the heart of the matter. Although formal sessions are effective for groups, some individuals open up more freely when the approach is less formal.

Our preference is to use the long-established, workshop-based approach to sweep up lessons at the end of the project and at any other formal review points. We recommend applying more informal techniques en route.

Informal techniques for collecting lessons learned

- *Top three survey.* When you're first introduced to someone who'll be involved in your project, ask for their top three pieces of advice. This is especially useful for gathering initial ideas at the start of your project or project stages.

▶

- *Initial quick survey by email.* Select a few individuals who are well placed to identify lessons – and who will warm to the task. Ask them to tell you the most important things they think the project should be doing more of and what needs to be done differently. This technique is useful at any point in your project.

- *Fireside chat.* Pick out the one or two people whose opinion you rate highly and have an informal session in relaxed surroundings. These one-to-ones are excellent for topics that might be sensitive or where frank views are required.

- *Lessons from your suppliers.* Ask your suppliers what typically goes wrong on the other projects they've worked on. Ask what you need to do differently to avoid these pitfalls. Consider doing this when you're planning or commissioning a new piece of work from anybody outside of your immediate team.

We refer to the techniques above as *lesson learned lite*. They're the simple, low-cost things a brilliant project manager should do *as a minimum*. Also because these techniques are low-key, they can easily be passed off as everyday enquiries where gathering lessons isn't the norm and is frowned upon.

We suggest you consider recording the lessons in a log, as and when they occur – just like the risks and issues log. You should record enough information to remind yourself at a future date about what happened and what you'd do differently or repeat. As this log grows, it will provide you with a set of handy hints for your personal use and plenty of ideas to bring along to more formal lessons learned sessions with your team.

Formal lessons learned sessions

Despite all the advantages of informal options, we remain keen supporters of the traditional, end-of-term type review that's synonymous with lessons learned. If you can assemble a representative cross-section of the project participants, and get them in the right frame of mind, they'll spark off each other and deliver exactly what the doctor ordered. At their best, there's no better way to get at the crux of what went well and what you could have done better.

Because of the diversity of people and opinions at these events, it's important to prepare thoroughly beforehand – just like any other important meeting or workshop. A meandering free-for-all simply won't deliver the important insights that will benefit you and your project.

In addition to your trusty facilitation techniques, you'll need to come equipped with some prompts to ensure a fruitful discussion. Our two favourites are widely used and rightly so. They have the added advantage of complementing each other nicely and give you the option of switching perspective if ideas are unexpectedly thin on the ground:

- *Project themes*: for example, people, processes and tools; or quality, resources and timescales.

- *Project stages*: for example, project initiation, requirements and design, construction, and project closure.

You'll also find these prompts come in useful for putting some structure around the lessons you capture.

Describing lessons

Even if you've done a brilliant job of capturing lessons, your success or failure in passing them on will hinge on how well you articulate what you've learned. You need to make sure you're offering good advice that's easy to understand and directly usable by your audience.

We have three golden rules when it comes to writing down the lessons themselves:

1   Lessons must contain specific, realistic, practical pieces of advice.

2   Lessons must conclude with recommended positive actions.

3   Lessons must be free from references to individuals.

Not only do you need to keep the lessons brief and focused, you also need to avoid overwhelming your audience with numerous observations. If you do this they won't take on board *anything* you've said. Imagine how memorable *one* isolated lesson would be compared with 100. No more than 10 lessons for maximum impact and less than 20 whatever happens. Keep focused on the big winners; this really is a case of less is more.

Normally there will be a healthy mix of different types of lessons. Some will be simple, quick wins that can be immediately applied. Others will require much more effort but provide a bigger payback. Some measures will be short-term, others permanent fixtures. If you don't end up with this kind of mix, it's worth taking another look to see whether you've missed anything important.

Even if you aren't planning on circulating your lessons more widely, we'd urge you to spend time documenting them in this way. The effort invested in distilling down and describing precisely what you've learned will sharpen your thinking. This will put you and your team in a much better position to benefit from your experiences.

Reusing and passing on lessons

Organisations aren't good at learning lessons because people aren't great at listening to advice, especially when it comes from one of their peers and it's unsolicited. So even if you're armed with a bunch of excellent lessons and you're feeling evangelical, remember to remain realistic about what you're likely to achieve. Even a brilliant project manager has to settle for sporadic success when it comes to passing on their hard-won lessons.

One thing's for certain: simply mailing out your lessons with a friendly note urging your colleagues to benefit from your experience will meet with an indifferent response. Perhaps you'll even unintentionally antagonise some of them, leaving them wondering, 'Who's this joker telling me how to do my job?'

Barker & Cole's top tips

Take an opportunistic approach to passing on your lessons. It's much easier to offer advice if you see one of your fellow project managers struggling with a difficult situation you grappled with previously.

Charity starts at home

Project managers – brilliant or otherwise – are not measured by their ability to pass on their lessons. For your own career success it's far more important that your lessons are reflected in improvements to the way you run your own projects. Without doubt, you'll be the keenest to benefit and anything else is an added plus.

In our experience, the most often repeated mistake is the failure to think hard enough about previous lessons at the start of a new project. It's like *Groundhog Day* because projects seem to begin with very little recollection of previous misdemeanours and good practice. However, it's at the start of a new project when all your previous, hard-won knowledge can be put to best use. Make sure you get the project team together for a day specifically dedicated to looking at lessons and factoring them into your current project.

One of the greatest challenges for a brilliant project manager is keeping the search for lessons on the everyday agenda. The big advantage of looking for lessons as you go is that you can often take advantage of them immediately. This becomes second nature after a while – making small adjustments to the way you and your team operate on the back of experience.

There are several ways to make the pursuit of lessons part of everyday project life. Our preferred option is to link this to the maintenance of the risk and issue log – where you are regularly thinking about what might go or has gone wrong. It's a small leap to consider what you could do better next time when things go wrong or to take note of good practice when a risk is neatly side-stepped.

Avoiding the major pitfalls

Gathering lessons should be a positive experience. However, if the exercise concentrates too much on where there was scope for improvement, there's a danger that an air of gloom will settle in. Teams can get obsessed with picking over the bones of a project and create the impression that nothing went right. In extreme circumstances even a project that was a rip-roaring success can be torn to shreds by an over-zealous lessons learned workshop – seizing defeat from the jaws of victory.

To combat this, it's essential to remind everyone that lessons are about the positive, not just the negative. Make sure your contributors spend time looking at what's gone well for the project. Set a positive mood by starting with a few judiciously chosen successes, as it also helps people to relax. Then end up with a few golden nuggets to close on an upbeat note. Remember this may well be the last public outing for your project team and leaving a final, positive impression can be as important as gathering useful lessons.

Occasionally, identifying lessons is seen as an opportunity to set the record straight with thinly veiled criticisms of *certain* people – especially when they are outside the team. This is counterproductive and must be avoided at all costs. Even when there's no malicious intent, it serves no practical purpose to name individuals or mention project-specific events. Generalising and depersonalising lessons is crucial, and it takes practice.

Start by removing named individuals, specify an action and home in on the root cause. For example, 'order all materials required by tradesmen well in advance and arrange delivery one week before they're due to start work' fits our criteria. Whereas, 'Norman Nobrains forgot to order nails for the carpenters and they wasted a morning waiting for an emergency delivery' does not.

Our final tip on avoiding major pitfalls is: chase quality, not quantity. A brilliant project manager should aim to capture the really important lessons – those that stand out from the everyday ifs-and-buts of any project. If you've collected lessons during the project, make sure you and the team sift through them and pick out the winners. If your lessons are defined in a workshop, call a halt when you can see that you're in danger of scraping the bottom of the barrel.

Summary

The traditional approach to lessons learned can look like a time-consuming and pointless business and, frankly, we agree wholeheartedly. Highlighting and advertising your mistakes – and nothing more – is at best pointless and at worst it's professional suicide. But it doesn't have to be that way and the judicious handling of the lessons learned process is one of the best ways to spot a brilliant project manager.

For a start, lessons are not just about mistakes, they should also include everything you've done well. For some strange reason project teams seem keen to draw attention to their mistakes, however trivial, yet seem almost reluctant to mention any good practice.

Gathering lessons requires an investment of time and resource that's pointless in isolation. No matter how clever or profound the lessons are, your outlay is repaid only if they are put to good use. The sole criterion for judging lessons should be how useful they prove to be. It's not about how big your report is, it's what you do with it that counts.

For lessons to flourish, projects need a healthy, blame-free culture where making mistakes is not the end of the world; a culture that encourages innovation and good practice. Steer the team away from vendettas and self-abuse.

Many project managers are sceptical about the value in identifying and using lessons. We think you'll be surprised by the *immediate* payback this can provide. Get your team together today and ask: what could we be doing better right now? After that, you won't need to be convinced about the longer-term benefits.

Barker & Cole's final word on *making use of lessons learned* ...

- Fear, blame, backstabbing and cover-ups are not just blockers for lessons, they'll undermine all aspects of your project.

- Don't try to avoid making mistakes *at all costs*. Just make sure you don't make the same mistakes twice.

- Cheer up! Don't forget that there are some things that went really well on your project. These are just as important.

- Don't overuse big set pieces. There's always time for 'lessons learned lite'.

- Don't get hung up about passing on lessons. Concentrate on using them yourself.

Chapter ten

the journey

to brilliant
project
management

fasten your seatbelts!

" Only dull people are brilliant at breakfast. "

Oscar Wilde (1854–1900)

What makes you brilliant?

So what makes a project manager brilliant? We believe it boils down to having an excellent understanding of management techniques, an aptitude for dealing with people and a commitment to continuous self-improvement. It's this combination and balance of skills that leads to one defining characteristic: brilliant project managers consistently deliver.

Brilliant project managers also prefer to specialise in a field or industry they know well. This experience often gives them a crucial advantage. It helps them to plan their projects, win the respect of their teams and avoid the pitfalls that go with the territory.

You don't need to be a genius to be a brilliant project manager but you do need to stick with good practice, build excellent working relationships and be prepared to learn lessons along the way.

Brilliant project managers are ...

- *Skilled in the core project management disciplines.* They know how to go about developing credible and robust project plans. They anticipate and deal effectively with adversity. They're adept at planning and managing their resources, and ensure what they deliver is fit-for-purpose.

▶

- *Talented at dealing with people.* They provide their teams with leadership and facilitate success day-by-day. However mundane it may seem, they also know how to run effective meetings and workshops.

- *Always keen to learn.* They recognise there's always room for improvement. They draw on their own experiences, and those of others, to improve their capabilities.

Preparing the ground for success

Brilliant project managers recognise the critical importance of preparation. This attitude extends into everything they do and say, whether it's having contingencies in place to deal with a serious project risk or circulating a well-constructed agenda in advance of a meeting.

Brilliant project managers make sure their projects are built on solid foundations, even if there's an urgency to get on with the *real work*. Sometimes this is easier said than done. It can take considerable strength of character to get the preparation right when you're under pressure to act immediately.

A vital part of the required groundwork is to be clear about what it takes to *keep the customer satisfied.* Innocent misunderstandings can easily go beyond points of fine detail and end up with significant differences in expectations. A brilliant project manager invests effort up-front to avoid creating a ticking time bomb.

Barker & Cole's home truths

Projects don't go wrong at the end. Even when it looks that way, the root cause will be found much earlier on.

Developing good habits

Project management is a people business. Brilliant project managers have a working style that gets the best out of their teams and builds the respect of customers and suppliers. Your attitude, and the way you behave, will play a big part in success or failure.

Seven habits of *brilliant project managers*

1 *Focusing on solutions to problems.* When you hit a problem, don't panic: slowly count to ten. Then give priority to resolving what's gone wrong, rather than looking for someone to blame.

2 *Being consultative yet decisive.* Involve your team in major decisions, but be prepared to make the final call.

3 *Remaining customer focused at all times.* Strive to see things through their eyes.

4 *Negotiating for a win–win result.* When you're horse trading ensure there's a positive outcome for everyone involved.

5 *Getting the best out of everyone.* Don't write off underachievers and make sure your star performers aren't coasting.

6 *Constantly looking to adapt and evolve.* Don't rest on your laurels. Be open-minded about what you can do better, even when all's gone according to plan.

7 *Leading by example.* Practise what you preach and work to the standards you want others to adopt. It's the best way to get your message across.

We're not suggesting you radically change your style and you should be able to develop these traits without too much difficulty. For some project managers getting the best out of people comes naturally. Others need to work on their behaviour until it becomes a habit.

Either way, for a brilliant project manager it's second nature to act in a way that nurtures self-belief and a winning attitude.

Good but not perfect

You'll set your own high standards, which will certainly be more than the bare minimum expected of you. However, even brilliant project managers know it's unrealistic to aim for perfection all of the time. You don't need to play a perfect game.

First, there simply aren't enough hours in the day to chase perfection all the time. Second, there's a knack to knowing when you need to stick to your guns and when to compromise. You'll be seen as inflexible if you don't make some concessions to pragmatism and risk sabotaging the good working relationships you're trying to build.

The key to success lies in spotting the times when the pursuit of excellence will give you the biggest possible payback. You also need to guard against gradually slipping into bad habits. Not having an agenda for a meeting or two is forgivable; never having one isn't.

Improving all the time

If you're going to become an even better project manager, you'll need to pinpoint your weaknesses and start to work on them. Get feedback from your team members, customers and suppliers to find out whether you're missing a trick or doing something counterproductive. Don't let the risk of a bruised ego stop you from asking for valuable pointers. After all, one weak spot may be enough to spoil an otherwise *brilliant* package.

Always look for opportunities to grow your experience. Use projects to sharpen up your core project management techniques and never miss a chance to practise your people skills. Finally, consider the other ways to extend your capabilities.

Brilliant development opportunities

- *Look for projects that will stretch you.* You'll learn little if you just stay within your comfort zone. Taking on a difficult project is great for your career development.

- *Show initiative by researching topics that are obvious 'gaps'.* There are publications covering everything you might want to know and plenty of freely available material on the internet.

- *See if you can find a mentor.* A little friendly, expert advice can go a long way. If you can't find a dedicated mentor, learn *on-the-job* from experienced people around you.

- *Take some formal training.* Use this to consolidate what you've learned through experience. You'll benefit both from the course material and from meeting other project managers.

If you're just starting out, or looking to plug some obvious gaps in your skill set, don't expect to become a brilliant project manager overnight. However, whether you're a novice or already an expert, you don't have to wait weeks to see a return on your efforts. There are plenty of techniques and tips you can put into use right away for immediate results – do something brilliant today.

It shouldn't happen to a project manager (but it did) . . .

At a social gathering, one project manager's wife let slip that her husband was never really off duty. Even jobs around the house were specified on a small card, estimated, costed and prioritised. When the project manager had any free time, job dockets were picked out in *consultation* with his wife. On finishing the work, actual costs and the time taken were recorded for later analysis.

Don't be brilliant all the time!

INDEX

Contents

		Questions	Answers

Introduction

Accounting for AQA: A-level year 2 Question Bank has been written to provide supplementary examination practice material for students of AQA's A-level year 2 in accounting.

The book is divided into two separate sections:

1 **Questions** appropriate for the AQA examinations, with gaps where students can write in the answers.

2 **Answers** to each of the questions, set out in the fully worked layout that should be used.

The book is also arranged in the chapter order of the main text book, **Accounting for AQA: A-level year 2** (see the Contents on the previous page).

Note that the assumption for this book is that AQA's A2-level specifications form year 2 of the two-year A-level course.

Alison Aplin

Accounting for AQA: A-level year 2

Question Bank

osborne
BOOKS

Alison Aplin

Published by Osborne Books Limited

Tel   01905 748071

Email   books@osbornebooks.co.uk
Website   www.osbornebooks.co.uk

Cover design by Windrush Group (www.windrushgroup.co.uk)

Printed by CPI Group (UK) Limited, Croydon, CR0 4YY

British Library Cataloguing in Publication Data

A catalogue record for this book is available from the British Library

ISBN: 978-1-911198-31-4

Use of accounting terminology

The AQA examinations in Accounting make full use of international terminology as set out in International Financial Reporting Standards (IFRSs). The following shows the international terminology, together with the terminology used previously.

International Terminology	Terminology used previously
Financial statements	
Appropriation account (partnership)	Profit and loss appropriation account
Cash and cash equivalents (limited companies)	Cash in hand, cash at bank/bank overdraft
Financial statements	Final accounts and balance sheets
Income statement	Trading and profit and loss account
Inventory	Stock
Irrecoverable debt	Bad debt
Loss for year	Net loss
Non-current assets	Fixed assets
Non-current liabilities	Long-term liabilities
Other payables	Expenses due; income received in advance
Other receivables	Expenses prepaid; income due
Profit for year	Net profit
Revenue (within an income statement)	Sales
Statement of financial position	Balance sheet
Trade payables	Trade creditors (creditors)
Trade receivables	Trade debtors (debtors)
Accounting ratios	
Expenses in relation to revenue %	Expenses in relation to sales %
Profit to revenue %	Net profit to sales %
Rate of inventory turnover	Rate of stock turnover
Trade payable days	Creditor payment period
Trade receivable days	Debtor collection period

Practice questions

FINANCIAL ACCOUNTING
QUESTIONS

CHAPTER 1: FINANCIAL STATEMENTS AND INTRODUCTION TO ETHICS

1.   From the statements below select whether they relate to financial accounting or management accounting:

Statements		Financial accounting	Management accounting
(a)	Reports are produced in a standard format, usually on an annual basis above transactions.		
(b)	The purpose of this type of accounting is to assist in decision-making, planning and control.		
(c)	Reports are produced to meet the needs of a business for the use of internal stakeholders.		
(d)	There is often a legal requirement to produce reports for this purpose.		

2.   Select the ethical principle which means that information about a business should not be disclosed to a third party:

A	Professional behaviour	
B	Objectivity	
C	Confidentiality	
D	Integrity	
E	Professional competence and due care	

3.   A cash payment of £47 for stationery has been posted in the accounts as £74.

Which of the following correctly describes the type of error and the corrections to be made?

Type of error		Entries to correct the error	
		Dr	Cr
A	Original entry	Stationery £47	Cash £47
		Cash £74	Stationery £74
B	Commission	Stationery £47	Cash £47
		Cash £74	Stationery £74
C	Original entry	Stationery £74	Cash £74
		Cash £47	Stationery £47
D	Commission	Stationery £74	Cash £74
		Cash £47	Stationery £47

4.   The accountant for Micha's Electricals Ltd has been preparing the financial statements for the year ended 31 March 20-8 and has discovered that an irrecoverable debt of £1,065 should have been written off.

Prior to making the above adjustment, the balances in the general ledger accounts at 31 March 20-8 were:

Trade receivables   £11,325

Provisions for doubtful debts   £608

The provisions for doubtful debts should be maintained at 5% of trade receivables.

After making the correct adjustments, the balance on the provisions for doubtful debts account will be:

A	£566	
B	£970	
C	£513	
D	£1,121	

5.   Oliver Limited prepares its financial statements to 31 May each year. At 31 May 20-8 its trial balance was as follows:

	Dr	Cr
	£000	£000
Administration expenses	485	
Issued share capital – ordinary shares		400
Trade and other receivables	610	
Cash and cash equivalents	207	
Share premium		100
Distribution expenses	79	
Plant and equipment at cost	2,160	
Depreciation on plant and equipment		757
Retained earnings at 1 June 20-7		577
Purchases	2,438	
Inventory at 1 June 20-7	75	
Trade and other payables		215
Revenue		3,803
Dividends paid	236	
Finance costs	27	
Long-term bank loan		465
	6,317	6,317

Notes:

- Inventory at 31 May 20-8 cost £79,000.

- The tax charge based on the profits for the year is £162,000.

- Depreciation on plant and equipment has already been provided for in the list of balances above and allocated to administration expenses.

Required:

Prepare the income statement, statement of changes in equity and statement of financial position of Oliver Limited for the year ended 31 May 20-8 in the next pages:

CHAPTER 2: INCOMPLETE RECORDS

1. Beth has the following assets and liabilities at 1 March 20-7:

	£
Office equipment	4,000
Motor vehicles	15,000
Inventory	6,500
Trade receivables	3,600
Trade payables	1,400
Bank overdraft	8,200

Calculate her opening capital at 1 March 20-7.

2. The following information was provided by Gary, a sole trader, for the year ended 30 September 20-8:

Capital at 1 October 20-7	£16,800
Capital at 30 September 20-8	£9,700
Profit for the year ended 30 September 20-8	£5,100

What were Gary's drawings for the year ended 30 September 20-8?

A	£7,100	
B	£12,200	
C	£2,000	
D	£21,400	

3.   Carys started a business on 1 January 20-8 and opened a new bank account on that date. A summary of her bank transactions for the year ended 31 December 20-8 were:

	£
Capital introduced	10,000
Payments to trade payables	26,510
Purchase of fixtures and fittings	14,000
Receipts from trade receivables	48,900
Drawings	7,800

Calculate her closing bank balance at 31 December 20-8.

4.   Kayo, a sole trader, has not maintained proper books of account. The following information is available relating to trade payables for the year ended 30 November 20-8:

Trade payables at 1 December 20-7	£13,800
Trade payables at 30 November 20-8	£15,650
Payments to trade payables	£147,300
Purchases returns	£438
Discounts received	£1,685

The figure for purchases for the year ended 30 November 20-8 was:

A	£165,073	
B	£149,503	
C	£147,573	
D	£151,273	

5.   The following information is available about wages paid for the year ended
      31 August 20-8:

Amounts owed to employees at 1 September 20-7	£600
Amounts owed to employees at 31 August 20-8	£900
Expense in the income statement	£56,500

How much was paid out of the bank in respect of wages for the year ended
31 August 20-8?

A	£56,200	
B	£56,800	
C	£56,500	
D	£57,100	

6.   A business has recently sold some equipment which cost £22,000 and had
      provision for depreciation at the time of sale of £14,000. The business made a
      profit on sale of £3,000.

      The sale proceeds were:

A	£25,000	
B	£5,000	
C	£8,000	
D	£11,000	

7.   Sales for the year are £500,000, the gross profit margin is 30%.

      Calculate the cost of sales.

      ----

8. Revenue for the year is £200,000, the gross profit mark-up is 25%, opening inventory is £15,000 and closing inventory is £20,000.

Purchases for the year are:

A	£160,000	
B	£150,000	
C	£165,000	
D	£155,000	

9. Jenny runs a florist and all takings are received in cash. Jenny banks the cash on a weekly basis after she has taken out any money required for cash payments.

Jenny has supplied the following information for the year:

Cash in the till at the start of the year	£450
Cash in the till at the end of the year	£500
Takings	£54,600
Bankings	£46,200
Cash payments	£7,600

During the year there was a break-in and some cash was stolen from the till.

Calculate the amount of cash that was stolen.

----

10. Bernard owns a stationery business; he does not keep proper books of account.

The following information is available for the year ended 31 December 20-8:

	1 January 20-8	31 December 20-8
	£	£
Inventory	14,250	18,910
Trade payables	5,600	7,850
Other payables – rent	0	1,000
Shop equipment at carrying value	56,800	41,700

A summary of the bank transactions for the year ended 31 December 20-8 are:

	Debit	Credit	Balance
	£	£	£
Balance at 1 January 20-8			8,968
Cash takings banked		336,236	345,204
Payments to trade payables	225,724		119,480
Drawings	42,000		77,480
Sale of equipment		680	78,160
Rent of shop	11,000		67,160
General expenses	15,326		51,834
Wages	44,000		7,834

- At 31 December 20-8 there are unpresented cheques to trade suppliers totalling £4,960 and amounts for cash takings not yet credited of £2,782.

- Bernard has taken some goods for his own use during the year, but he is unsure of the value of these goods.

- All purchases are made on credit and all sales are on a cash basis.

- The equipment sold during the year had a net book value of £1,200.

- Bernard's policy is to have a mark-up on all goods sold of 50%.

Required:

(a)   Calculate the opening capital at 1 January 20-8 for Bernard.

(b)   Prepare the trading section of the business's income statement for the year ended 31 December 20-8 to show the value of goods taken for own use by Bernard.

(c)   Complete the income statement for the year ended 31 December 20-8 to show Bernard's profit or loss for the year.

(d)   Prepare the statement of financial position for Bernard at 31 December 20-8.

CHAPTER 3: COMPUTER ACCOUNTING

1. From the statements below select whether each is an advantage or disadvantage of a computerised accounting system:

Statements	Advantage	Disadvantage
(a) Knowledge of double-entry bookkeeping is not required.		
(b) Users may not fully understand processes and errors are likely to occur.		
(c) Most transactions only need to be input once, therefore time is saved.		
(d) Reports can be produced automatically and tailored to the needs of a business.		

2. Bow Ltd is considering moving to a computerised accounting system. What costs could Bow Ltd incur?

----

3.   Progress Ltd is planning to introduce an integrated computer accounting system. The operations director has been told about all the advantages by the software company but is anxious to know about the possible disadvantages.

You are to state two possible disadvantages of this proposal and explain how they could cause problems within the company.

Disadvantage 1

Disadvantage 2

4. Describe one benefit and one drawback of using spreadsheets to produce financial information.

Benefit of using spreadsheets

Drawback of using spreadsheets

CHAPTER 4: PARTNERSHIP FINANCIAL STATEMENTS

1. Select whether the following statements are true or false about the Partnership Act 1890:

Statements	True	False
(a) Profits or losses are shared in the same proportion as the capital which has been contributed by each partner.		
(b) No partner is entitled to any drawings.		
(c) Partners may be entitled to a salary.		
(d) Partners are not entitled to receive interest on their capital.		

2. Mike and Bryan are in partnership, sharing profits on an equal basis. Any drawings are charged interest at 5% per annum, Mike had drawings of £12,000 during the year and Bryan had none.

Partnership profits for the year were £53,400; Mike and Bryan will each receive a share of the remaining profits of:

A	£26,700	
B	£27,000	
C	£26,400	
D	£32,700	

3. In the first year of a partnership, the following information is available about one of the partners, Margaret:

Drawings	£15,000
Salary	£16,000
Interest on drawings	£300
Interest on capital	£2,250
Share of profit	£19,000

What is the balance on Margaret's current account at the end of the year?

A	£21,950	
B	£22,550	
C	£36,950	
D	£18,050	

4. Alison, Bernadette and Coleen are in partnership and share profits on the following basis:

	Alison	Bernadette	Coleen
Salary	£10,000	£nil	£20,000
Share of profits	30%	50%	20%

They are also entitled to interest on their capital accounts of 3% per annum. The capital account balances at the start of the year were:

	Alison	Bernadette	Coleen
Capital	£10,000	£30,000	£10,000

The partnership profit for the year ended 31 March 20-8 was £66,500.

Prepare the partnership appropriation account for Alison, Bernadette and Coleen for the year ended 31 March 20-8, on the next page.

5.   Eliza and Sam are in partnership called 'ES Hairdressers'.

The following information is available for the year ended 31 December 20-8:

	Eliza	Sam
	£	£
Capital accounts at 1 January 20-8	40,000 Cr	30,000 Cr
Current accounts at 1 January 20-8	480 Dr	1,310 Cr
Drawings	12,000	28,640
Partnership salary	8,000	0
Interest on drawings	600	1,432
Interest on capital	2,400	1,800

The remaining profits are shared in the ratio of 60% to Eliza and 40% to Sam.

The partnership profit for the year ended 31 December 20-8 was £41,268.

Prepare the partners' capital and current accounts for the year ended 31 December 20-8:

6. Ayesha and Josh are in partnership running a bookshop called 'Obscure Fiction'. The following trial balance has been taken from their accounts for the year ended 31 March 20-8:

	Dr £	Cr £
Capital account: Ayesha		25,000
Capital account: Josh		25,000
Current account: Ayesha	450	
Current account: Josh		180
Drawings: Ayesha	6,845	
Drawings: Josh	13,050	
Purchases	36,750	
Revenue		79,800
Opening inventory	5,865	
Wages	7,380	
Rent and rates	8,300	
Sundry expenses	585	
Discounts received		524
Credit card charges	880	
Motor expenses	689	
Equipment at carrying value	24,800	
Trade payables		2,890
Bank	27,800	
	133,394	133,394

Notes at 31 March 20-8:

- Inventory was valued at £6,273.

- Wages owing were £56.

- Prepaid rent was £500.

- Depreciation is to be charged on the equipment at 25% per annum, using the reducing balance method.

- Josh is to receive a partnership salary of £6,000.

- Interest is to be allowed on partners' capital accounts at 5% per annum, there is no interest on partners' drawings.

- Remaining profits and losses are to be shared equally.

Required:

Prepare the income statement, partners' capital and current accounts and statement of financial position of Obscure Fiction for the year ended 31 March 20-8.

CHAPTER 5: CHANGES IN PARTNERSHIPS

1.   From the statements below select the one which is correct about goodwill:

(a)	Goodwill is the net assets of a business, the assets less liabilities.	
(b)	Goodwill is the amount that is contributed into a business by the owners.	
(c)	Goodwill is the difference between the value of a business and the net value of its separate assets and liabilities.	
(d)	Goodwill is the total value of non-current assets owned by a business.	

2.   Annie, Bertie and Clive are in partnership and Bertie decides to retire. The agreed valuation of goodwill is £50,000 and the profit sharing ratios are:

	Old profit sharing ratio	New profit sharing ratio
Annie	40%	60%
Bertie	40%	
Clive	20%	40%

The goodwill adjustments in Clive's capital account are:

A	Dr £30,000,	Cr £20,000	
B	Dr £NIL,	Cr £20,000	
C	Dr £10,000,	Cr £20,000	
D	Dr £20,000,	Cr £10,000	

3.   Donald is retiring from a partnership, he has a balance on his capital account of £30,000 and is paid £50,000 from the partnership bank account on the date he retires. Donald's share of the goodwill created at the date of his retirement is £45,000. Any remaining balance on Donald's capital will be transferred to a loan account.

How much will the partnership owe to Donald in the form of a loan?

A	£Nil	
B	£25,000	
C	£35,000	
D	£75,000	

4.   Drita and Elizabeth are in partnership sharing profits 50:50, they each have a balance on their capital accounts of £30,000.

Fred joins the partnership and introduces £50,000 into the bank. The new profit sharing ratio is:

Drita	60%
Elizabeth	20%
Fred	20%

Goodwill has an agreed valuation of £64,000 and non-current assets have been revalued, creating a surplus of £15,600. It has been agreed that a goodwill account is not to be maintained in the books of account.

Prepare the partners' capital accounts, after the above transactions have taken place.

5.   The following information is available about the 'IT for Novices' partnership for the year ended 31 December 20-8:

- The partners at the beginning of the year were Xaviar and Yan.

- Zain joined the partnership on 1 April 20-8.

- Partners' annual salaries:

	£
Xaviar	18,000
Yan	24,000
Zain	12,000

- Partners' interest on capital (for a full year):

	£
Xaviar	960
Yan	840
Zain	600

- Profit share to 31 March 20-8:

	%
Xaviar	70
Yan	30

- Profit share from 1 April 20-8:

	%
Xaviar	60
Yan	20
Zain	20

The profit for the year ended 31 December 20-8 was £120,000.

Prepare the partnership appropriation account for the year ended 31 December 20-8.

6.   Peggy and Nora are in partnership trading as 'Our Local Café' and Queenie joined the partnership on 1 January 20-8. The following trial balance has been taken from their accounts for the year ended 31 December 20-8:

	Dr	Cr
	£	£
Capital introduced: Queenie		44,500
Capital account at 1 Jan 20-8: Peggy		15,000
Capital account at 1 Jan 20-8: Nora		15,000
Current account at 1 Jan 20-8: Peggy		580
Current account at 1 Jan 20-8: Nora		630
Drawings: Peggy	33,000	
Drawings: Nora	32,000	
Drawings: Queenie	17,000	
Purchases	151,438	
Revenue		266,700
Opening inventory	10,200	
Wages	29,200	
Office costs	10,196	
Sundry expenses	1,386	
Property	30,000	
Trade payables		15,560
Bank	43,550	
	357,970	357,970

Notes at 31 December 20-8:

- Inventory was valued at £15,300.

- Peggy took goods for her own use totalling £750.

- On 1 January 20-8 the property was revalued at £50,000 and goodwill was valued at £65,000, neither of these transactions have been reflected in the accounts. Goodwill is not to be maintained in the books of account.

- All profits were shared 50/50 between Peggy and Nora.

- The new profit sharing ratio is Peggy (40%), Nora (40%), Queenie (20%).

Required:

Prepare the income statement, partners' capital and current accounts and statement of financial position of 'Our Local Café' for the year ended 31 December 20-8.

CHAPTER 6: ACCOUNTING FOR LIMITED COMPANIES

1.   International Accounting Standard (IAS) 1 states that a complete set of financial statements should include:

		True	False
(a)	Statement of changes in equity		
(b)	Statement of cash flows		
(c)	Auditors' report		
(d)	Income statement		
(e)	Appropriation account		
(f)	Statement of financial position		
(g)	Statement of affairs		
(h)	Accounting policies and explanatory notes		

2.   From the definitions below, select the one that correctly describes the accruals accounting concept:

(a)	Financial statements should not include the personal expenses or income or, record personal assets and liabilities for any of the people involved in owning or running a company.	
(b)	Only transactions which can be measured in monetary terms can be included in the financial records or statements.	
(c)	Financial statements should take a conservative approach where there is any doubt in the reporting of profits or the valuation of assets.	
(d)	Financial statements are prepared on the basis that income and expenses occurring in the same accounting period are matched.	

3. Select whether the following statements are true or false about limited company accounts:

Statements	True	False
(a) A copy of the management accounts must be filed with Companies House.		
(b) Private limited companies must file statutory accounts with Companies House within six months of the end of their accounting period.		
(c) The accounts of all companies must be audited by external auditors, who are appointed by the shareholders and form an opinion on the company's financial statements.		
(d) The legal and regulatory framework sets out the rules which must be followed when preparing limited company accounts.		

4. Terry has just been appointed as a director of a limited company.

(a) Briefly state the responsibilities of directors under the Companies Act 2006.

(b) List the items that should be contained within the directors' report which is included in the published accounts of a company.

5.   Suggest two external and two internal stakeholders of a limited company and state why they may be interested in the financial statements.

External stakeholders

Internal stakeholders

6.   List and explain two benefits and two limitations of published accounts.

Benefits

_____

_____

_____

_____

_____

_____

_____

_____

Limitations

_____

_____

_____

_____

_____

_____

_____

7. Q Ltd has the following information available about its share capital:

	£
Authorised capital – Ordinary shares of 25p each	250,000
Issued capital – Ordinary shares of 25p each	200,000

Q Ltd has offered all existing shareholders' a rights issue at 50p per share on the basis of one new share for every eight held.

Assuming that all shareholders take up the rights issue, Q Ltd will receive:

A	£25,000	
B	£50,000	
C	£62,500	
D	£31,250	

8. The equity section of the statement of financial position of Georgie Ltd at 1 January 20-8 is shown below:

	£
Ordinary shares of 10p each, fully paid	300,000
Share premium	50,000
Retained earnings	41,000
Total equity	391,000

On 1 April 20-8, a bonus issue was completed. The shares were issued on the basis of one new share for every five shares held.

During the year ended 31 December 20-8 land and building were revalued with an increase of £200,000, dividends paid were £240,000 and the profit for the year was £285,000.

At the end of the year a final dividend of £63,000 was proposed.

Prepare the statement of changes in equity of Georgie Ltd for the year ended 31 December 20-8.

9. The directors of Fitness plc have provided the following statement of financial position extracts:

	31 May 20-7	31 May 20-8
	£000	£000
Non-current assets carrying amounts:		
Land and buildings	225	343
Plant and equipment	188	240
	413	583

Additional information:

- Land and buildings were revalued at £350,000 on 1 June 20-7, their original cost was £250,000.

- Land and buildings are depreciated using the straight-line method at 2% per annum.

- The cost of plant and equipment at 1 June 20-7 was £425,000.

- In the year to 31 May 20-8, plant and equipment which had originally cost £40,000 was sold. The depreciation charge on these non-current assets was £10,000.

- In the year to 31 May 20-8, plant and equipment was purchased at a cost of £162,000.

- Plant and equipment are depreciated using the reducing balance method at 25% per annum.

Complete the detailed note for the published accounts of Fitness plc for the year ended 31 May 20-8, which shows the movement in the carrying amounts of land and buildings and plant and equipment, using the template provided on the next page:

Fitness plc

Non-current assets note for the year ended 31 May 20-8

	Land and buildings	Plant and equipment	Total
	£000	£000	£000
Cost			
At 1 June 20-7			
Additions at cost			
Less Cost of disposals			
Revaluation			
	———	———	———
At 31 May 20-8			
	———	———	———
Depreciation			
At 1 June 20-7			
Charge for the year			
Less Eliminated on disposal			
Less Eliminated on revaluation			
	———	———	———
At 31 May 20-8			
	———	———	———
	———	———	———
Carrying amount at 31 May 20-8			
	———	———	———

10. Victor Ltd prepares its financial statements to 31 March each year. At 31 March 20-8 its trial balance was as follows:

	Dr	Cr
	£000	£000
Administration expenses	131	
Ordinary shares of £1 each, fully paid		300
Trade and other receivables	194	
Bank overdraft		48
Share premium		150
Distribution expenses	122	
Finance costs	2	
Property cost	380	
Plant and equipment cost	750	
Depreciation on plant and equipment		485
Retained earnings at 1 April 20-7		107
Purchases	484	
Inventory at 1 April 20-7	57	
Trade and other payables		82
Revenue		1,084
Dividends paid	136	
	2,256	2,256

Further information:

- Inventory was valued at £65,000 on 31 March 20-8.

- Irrecoverable debts of £17,000 are to be written-off to administration expenses.

- The tax charge based on the profits for the year is £35,000.

- The property is to be revalued to £450,000.

- Depreciation of plant and equipment is to be provided for the year at 20% on a straight-line basis and is to be apportioned equally to administration expenses and distribution expenses.

Required:

Prepare the income statement, statement of changes in equity and statement of financial position of Victor Ltd for the year ended 31 March 20-8.

CHAPTER 7: STATEMENT OF CASH FLOWS

1. Which of the following statements correctly describes the types of inflows and outflows that are included in the financing section of a statement of cash flows:

(a) The changes in cash and cash equivalents for the period.	
(b) The main revenue producing activities and the payments of interest and tax.	
(c) Receipts from the issue of new shares, payments to repay share capital, changes in non-current liabilities and the payment of dividends.	
(d) The purchase and sale of non-current assets and other investments, and interest and dividends received.	

2. Pete Ltd has the following information relating to the year ended 30 November 20-8:

	£
Loss from operations	6,846
Depreciation	5,064
Loss on sale of non-current assets	782
Decrease in inventory	2,889
Increase in trade receivables	3,015
Increase in trade payables	2,930

The cash from operating activities included in the statement of cash flows is:

A	£15,496	
B	£(1,000)	
C	£(3,804)	
D	£1,804	

3. The following information has been extracted from the statement of financial position of Hood Ltd for the year ended 31 December 20-8:

	31 December 20-8	31 December 20-7
	£	£
Current assets – Bank	9,084	–
Current liabilities – Bank overdraft	–	5,127
Non-current liabilities – Bank loan	55,685	52,134

The net increase/(decrease) in cash and cash equivalents included in the statement of cash flows for the year ended 31 December 20-8 is:

A	£(14,211)	
B	£(10,660)	
C	£10,660	
D	£14,211	

4. Trent Ltd has the following activities for the year ended 31 October 20-8:

	£
Proceeds from the sale of non-current assets	8,500
Receipts from the issue of share capital	102,000
Purchase of non-current assets	86,000
Repayment of non-current loans	5,000
Dividends paid	27,600
Dividends received	1,200

The figure for investing activities included in the statement of cash flows is:

A	£(76,300)	
B	£69,400	
C	£(6,900)	
D	£(103,900)	

5. Perry Ltd has the following information for the year ended 30 June 20-8:

	£
Proceeds from the sale of non-current assets	6,200
Receipts from the issue of share capital	10,250
Purchase of non-current assets	2,500
Increase in non-current loans	6,000
Dividends paid	15,000
Interest received	750

The figure for financing activities included in the statement of cash flows is:

A	£4,450	
B	£5,700	
C	£1,250	
D	£4,250	

6. Extracts from the statement of financial position of Daffodil Ltd regarding property, plant and equipment (PPE) for the year ended 31 March 20-8 are as follows:

	31 March 20-8	31 March 20-7
PPE – carrying amount	£63,107	£57,248

The income statement includes the following:

	31 March 20-8
PPE – depreciation	£7,283
Profit on sale of non-current assets	£250

During the year property, plant and equipment was disposed of with a carrying amount of £1,800.

Calculate the figures for proceeds from the sale of non-current assets and purchase of non-current assets to be included in the statement of cash flows for the year ended 31 March 20-8.

7.   The statement of financial position of Ninety Ltd for the last two years are:

Statement of Financial Position as at 31 December 20-8

	20-8		20-7	
	£000	£000	£000	£000
Non-current assets				
Cost	8,570		7,825	
Depreciation to date	(1,569)	7,001	(1,321)	6,504
Current assets				
Inventory	118		129	
Trade receivables	333		301	
Cash and equivalents	64		107	
		515		537
TOTAL ASSETS		7,516		7,041
EQUITY				
Ordinary shares		1,700		1,500
Share premium		280		250
Retained earnings		4,162		4,275
TOTAL EQUITY		6,142		6,025
Non-current liabilities				
Loans		1,002		687
Current liabilities				
Trade payables	94		78	
Tax liability	278		251	
		372		329
		7,516		7,041

Further information:

• Additional non-current assets were purchased at a cost of £784,000.

• Non-current assets, which had been depreciated by £28,000 were sold for £14,000.

- There were no other disposals or purchases of non-current assets.

- Taxation paid totalled £353,000.

- Dividends paid totalled £1,386,000.

- The income statement for the year ended 31 December 20-8 included:

  depreciation charges £276,000

  finance costs £152,000

  taxation provision £380,000

Required:

Prepare the statement of cash flows for Ninety Ltd for the year ended 31 December 20-8.

CHAPTER 8: INTERPRETATION OF ACCOUNTING INFORMATION

Use the information below about Whitey plc to answer questions 1 to 5:

Current market price per share	£4.80
Profit for the year before interest and tax	£630,000
Profit for the year after tax	£450,000
Dividend on ordinary shares for the year	£360,000
Number of issued ordinary shares of £1 each	300,000
Interest payable for the year	£20,000

1. The dividend yield of Whitey plc is:

A	25.00%	
B	31.25%	
C	43.75%	
D	80.00%	

2. The earnings per share of Whitey plc is:

A	£1.20	
B	£1.50	
C	£2.10	
D	£3.80	

3. The dividend cover of Whitey plc is:

A	1.25 times	
B	1.50 times	
C	1.75 times	
D	4.00 times	

4.   The price earnings of Whitey plc is:

A	1.25	
B	3.20	
C	4.00	
D	4.80	

5.   The interest cover of Whitey plc is:

A	1.25 times	
B	1.75 times	
C	22.50 times	
D	31.50 times	

6.   Which of the following statements correctly defines liquidity?

(a)	The financial stability of a business on a long-term basis.	
(b)	A measure of the surplus of income over expenditure against either revenue or capital employed.	
(c)	The financial stability of a business on a short-term basis.	
(d)	The effective and efficient use of assets and liabilities.	

7. Marina has recently won some money and she has decided to invest in one of two companies. Marina has decided to calculate financial ratios based on the information from the financial statements she has received about the two companies.

   Discuss the limitations of using financial ratios to make this investment decision.

8.   The financial statements for Calvin Ltd for the last two years are as follows:

Calvin Ltd

Income Statement for the year ended 30 April 20-8

	20-8		20-7	
	£000	£000	£000	£000
Revenue		10,800		5,600
Opening inventory	652		350	
Purchases	7,994		3,942	
	8,646		4,292	
Less Closing inventory	654		652	
Cost of sales		7,992		3,640
Gross profit		2,808		1,960
Less Expenses:				
Administration expenses	1,202		813	
Distribution expenses	120		65	
		1,322		878
Profit for the year from operations		1,486		1,082
Less Finance costs		190		18
Profit for the year before tax		1,296		1,064
Less Tax		260		210
Profit for the year after tax		1,036		854

Calvin Ltd

Statement of Financial Position as at 30 April 20-8

	20-8		20-7	
	£000	£000	£000	£000
Non-current assets				
Plant and equipment		1,050		1,100
Current assets				
Inventory	654		652	
Trade receivables	2,850		950	
Cash and equivalents	–		780	
		3,504		2,382
TOTAL ASSETS		4,554		3,482
EQUITY				
Ordinary shares		1,200		1,200
Retained earnings		156		837
TOTAL EQUITY		1,356		2,037
Non-current liabilities				
Loans		498		805
Current liabilities				
Bank overdraft	690		–	
Trade payables	1,750		430	
Tax liability	260		210	
		2,700		640
		4,554		3,482

Required:

Calculate the following ratios for the year ended 30 April 20-8 for Calvin Ltd in the table below (the ones for the previous year have already been entered):

Ratio	30 April 20-8	30 April 20-7
Gross profit margin		35%
Profit in relation to revenue		19%
Return on capital employed		38.07%
Interest cover		60.11 times
Current ratio		3.72 : 1
Liquid capital ratio		2.7 : 1
Trade receivables days		61.92 days
Trade payable days		39.81 days
Rate of inventory turnover days		50.24 days
Capital gearing		28.33%

Workings:

9. Mike is considering investing in Calvin Ltd. Using the financial statements and the ratios you calculated in the previous question, along with the ratios from the previous year, write a report to Mike recommending whether or not he should invest in Calvin Ltd.

REPORT	
To:	Mike
From:	AQA accounting student
Subject:	Potential investment in Calvin Ltd
Date:	Today

10. Turkish Baths plc made a profit from operations of £3,860,000 in the year ended 31 March 20-8, however the statement of financial position shows that the bank account at the start of the year was £625,000 and at the end of the year was overdrawn by £107,000.

Ian, a shareholder, would like an explanation of the reasons for the difference between the two figures and has supplied you with the statement of cash flows below:

Turkish Baths plc

Statement of Cash Flows for the year ended 31 March 20-8

	£000	£000
Profit from operations		3,860
Depreciation		516
Increase in inventory		(502)
Increase in trade receivables		(368)
Increase in trade payables		31
Cash from operating activities		**3,537**
Interest paid		(31)
Tax paid		(740)
Net cash from operating activities		**2,766**
Investing activities		
Purchase of non-current assets	(2,584)	
Net cash used in investing activities		**(2,584)**
Financing activities		
Decrease in non-current loans	(580)	
Dividends paid	(334)	
Net cash used in financing activities		**(914)**
Net decrease in cash and cash equivalents		**(732)**
Cash and cash equivalents at the start of the year		625
Cash and cash equivalents at the end of the year		(107)

Required:

Explain to Ian the differences between profit from operations and the fall in the bank balance of Turkish Baths plc for the year ended 31 March 20-8.

CHAPTER 9: ACCOUNTING REGULATIONS AND ETHICS

1. The legal and regulatory framework of the accounting sector includes:

		True	False
(a)	Accounting standards		
(b)	Company law		
(c)	UK's Corporate Governance Code		
(d)	Conceptual Framework for Financial Reporting		

2. An office junior has told a partner that she can prepare payroll records for a client. You know that she is related to the director of the client company.

    The fundamental principle of ethical behaviour threatened by this situation is:

A	Integrity	
B	Objectivity	
C	Professional competence and due care	
D	Professional behaviour	

3.   Sam has worked in practice for many years, however, he is not familiar with the law relating to insolvency and has consulted a legal expert about a specific client.

This is an example of:

A	Integrity	
B	Confidentiality	
C	Professional competence and due care	
D	Objectivity	

4.   An accountant has prepared the financial statements of a limited company who employs him. The managing director has told the accountant, "unless you increase the figure for purchases, your job will be on the line".

This is an example of:

A	a self-interest threat	
B	an intimidation threat	
C	a self-review threat	
D	a familiarity threat	

5.   The Consultative Committee of Accountancy Bodies (CCAB) includes:

A	Her Majesty's Revenue and Customs (HMRC)	
B	Financial Reporting Council (FRC)	
C	Association of Chartered Certified Accountants (ACCA)	
D	Chartered Institute of Management Accountants (CIMA)	

6. State three safeguards which have been introduced by the accountancy profession, legislation or accountancy regulations to guard against threats to fundamental ethical principles.

----

7. List two examples of Corporate Social Responsibility policies a large company may wish to adopt.

----

8.   Explain the steps that an accountant in practice should take to deal with unethical or illegal acts committed by a client.

MANAGEMENT ACCOUNTING
QUESTIONS

CHAPTER 10: MANAGEMENT ACCOUNTING: THE USE OF BUDGETS

1. From the statements below identify which ones relate to management accounting:

(a)	Reports are in a set format which are often required by law.	
(b)	Reports are based on the recent past and projections for the future.	
(c)	Reports are produced to aid decision making, planning and control.	
(d)	Reports are used primarily for internal purposes.	

2. Select the correct definition of a budget from the statements below:

(a)	The difference between expected and actual revenues or costs.	
(b)	The period of time it takes for the initial cost of an investment to be repaid from net cash inflows.	
(c)	A financial plan for a business which is prepared in advance and generally covers a period of up to 12 months.	
(d)	A costing method which identifies what causes overheads to be incurred.	

3.   The following information is available from Sheffield Steel Ltd, a manufacturer of steel rods:

	Month 1 (units)	Month 2 (units)
Sales	6,240	7,860
Opening inventory	1,560	

The closing inventory should be maintained at 25% of the following month's sales.

The production budget for month 1 is:

A	5,835 units	
B	4,680 units	
C	8,205 units	
D	6,645 units	

4.   Hippy Ltd started to trade on 1 July and has the following budgeted credit purchases:

July	£21,000
August	£23,000

50% of trade payables will be paid in the month of purchase and a 2% cash discount will be deducted.

The remainder of trade payables will be paid in the month after purchase, with no cash discount.

The amount to be paid in August to trade payables is:

A	£22,540	
B	£21,770	
C	£22,000	
D	£21,560	

5. Each unit of product S requires 3.5 labour hours.

The number of units of product S required to be produced in May is 300.

There are 1,000 labour hours available for product S in May.

Calculate the surplus or shortfall of labour hours for the month of May for product S.

6.   Beverley Ltd sells memory sticks at a unit price of £15.50. The sales manager has predicted sales for the next six months to be:

January	800 units
February	As January with a 10% increase
March	As January with a 10% increase
April	As March with a 5% decrease
May	As January
June	As May with a 15% increase

Calculate the sales units and sales values for memory sticks for the next six months and enter them into the table below.

	Jan	Feb	Mar	Apr
Units				
	£	£	£	£
Sales				

	May	Jun	Total
Units			
	£	£	£
Sales			

7. The following budgeted information is available about product C34:

- Standard material usage per unit is 3 kg.

- Budgeted sales per month:

Month 1	500 units
Month 2	600 units
Month 3	560 units
Month 4	650 units
Month 5	600 units

- Opening inventory at the start of month 1 of finished units is 125.

- Each month's closing inventory of finished units is to be 25% of the following month's sales, however, the maximum capacity in the warehouse is 160 units.

- Opening inventory at the start of month 1 of materials is 315 kg.

- Each month's closing inventory of materials is to be maintained at one fifth of the following month's production.

- The required materials for production in month 5 is estimated at 1,830 kg.

- The cost per kg of material is £0.50.

Complete the table on the following page to calculate the cost of material purchases for product C34 for months 1 to 4.

	Month 1	Month 2	Month 3	Month 4
Production budget	Units	Units	Units	Units
Sales				
Opening inventory				
Closing inventory				
Production				
Purchases budget	kg	kg	kg	kg
Production				
Opening inventory				
Closing inventory				
Purchases				
Purchases budget	£	£	£	£
Purchases				

Workings:

8. Sis Ltd makes sales to its customers on credit. The following information is available for April to June:

   - Budgeted credit sales:

April	£30,000
May	£37,500
June	£45,000

   - 40% of trade receivables pay in the month of sale, taking advantage of a 3% cash discount which is available.

   - The remainder of trade receivables pay in the following month and do not receive a cash discount. However, 5% of these will never pay and should be regarded as irrecoverable debts.

   - Trade receivables at 1 April are £16,800.

   Complete the table below to calculate receipts from trade receivables for April to June for Sis Ltd:

	April	May	June
Receipts:	£	£	£
Month of sale			
Less Discount			
Month after sale			
Less Irrecoverable debts			
Total			

   Workings:

9.   Alistair runs a business called 'The IT Shop' and is considering expanding. He has asked you to produce a cash budget for the next three months based on his plan and has provided the following information:

   • The bank balance at 1 January 20-8 is £5,866.

   • Budgeted sales for the next three months are:

	Cash (£)	Credit (£)
January	1,500	23,000
February	1,600	24,000
March	1,650	26,000

   • 30% of credit customers pay in the month of sale, taking advantage of a 3% cash discount which is available.

   • 40% of credit customers pay in the month after sale, with the remainder paying in the following month.

   • Trade receivables at 1 January 20-8 are:

	£	
November sales	4,800	
December sales	11,900	(£6,800 is expected in January)
Total	16,700	

   • All purchases are made on credit and paid for in the following month, purchases forecasts are:

	£
January	5,750
February	6,000
March	6,500

   • Trade payables at 1 January 20-8 are £4,250.

   • The cost of a major shop refit is £28,000 and this will be paid for in February.

   • Operating expenses total £3,600 per month and Alistair's drawings are £1,800 per month; both are paid for in the month they are incurred.

(a)   Prepare a cash budget for 'The IT Shop' for the period ended 31 March 20-8:

	January	February	March
	£	£	£

(b)   Alistair has an existing overdraft agreement with the bank for £1,000. He would like to know whether he should apply to the bank for an increase in the limit.

Based on the cash budget you have prepared, advise Alistair on whether he needs to increase his overdraft limit.

----

10. Further information about 'The IT Shop' is:

- Opening inventory at 1 January 20-8 is £1,684.

- Closing inventory at 31 March 20-8 is estimated to be £2,400.

- Non-current assets at 1 January 20-8 are £5,000.

- The depreciation charge for the three months ended 31 March 20-8 is estimated to be £1,500 (this includes the charge for the shop refit).

- Opening capital at 1 January 20-8 is £25,000.

Required:

Prepare the budgeted income statement and budgeted statement of financial position of 'The IT Shop' for the period ended 31 March 20-8, based on the above information and the figures provided and calculated in question 9.

CHAPTER 11: ABSORPTION AND ACTIVITY BASED COSTING

1. Select the correct definition of a cost centre from the statements below:

(a)	Units of output to which costs can be charged.
(b)	Groups of overhead costs that are incurred by the same activity.
(c)	Sections of a business to which costs can be charged.
(d)	Activities which cause costs to be incurred.

2. From the statements below select whether they relate to marginal, absorption or activity based costing:

Statements	Marginal	Absorption	Activity based
(a) Overheads are attributed to production on the basis of activities.			
(b) Costs are classified as either fixed or variable.			
(c) The overhead absorption rate is usually calculated using direct labour hours or machine hours.			
(d) The cost of producing one extra unit of output can be identified.			

3.   The following information is available about product X:

	£
Total direct material cost	450
Total direct labour cost	510
Overheads	480

150 units of product X are produced.

The absorption cost of producing one unit of product X is:

A	£3.20	
B	£6.20	
C	£6.40	
D	£9.60	

4.   The following information is available about product Y:

Selling price per unit	£12.00
Direct material per unit	£2.25
Direct labour per unit	£1.50
Total fixed production overhead	£50,000
Number of units	20,000

The marginal cost of producing one unit of product Y is:

A	£3.75	
B	£5.75	
C	£6.25	
D	£8.25	

5.   The following information is available about product Z:

Selling price per unit   £100
Variable cost per unit   £45
Total fixed costs   £88,000
Budgeted production   2,400 units

How many units of Product Z must be sold to produce a profit of £22,000?

A	880 units	
B	1,100 units	
C	1,600 units	
D	2,000 units	

6.   Alpha Kite Ltd uses cost-plus pricing to calculate the selling prices of its products, based on a 25% mark-up on absorption cost.

The following information is available about product D11:

Prime cost per unit   £360
Fixed overhead per unit   £40

The selling price per unit of product D11 should be set at:

A	£450	
B	£480	
C	£500	
D	£534	

7.   Alpine Coatings Ltd manufactures two products, the Honey Dew and the Sunflower.

The following information is available about the two products:

	Honey Dew	Sunflower
Selling price per unit	£18.00	£22.50
Direct material per unit	£7.40	£8.50
Direct labour per unit	£1.80	£3.60
Monthly production	4,000 units	6,000 units

Alpine Coatings Ltd's total monthly factory overheads are £80,000 and activity based costing is used to absorb the overheads, using the information below:

Cost pool	Overhead per month	Cost driver	Details for each product
Machinery set-ups	£66,000	Number of times machinery is set-up during production	Honey Dew – 3 set-ups per unit produced Sunflower – 8 set-ups per unit produced
Quality inspections	£14,000	Number of times products are inspected during production	Honey Dew – 1 inspection per unit produced Sunflower – 4 inspections per unit produced

Calculate the cost per unit and the profit or loss per unit for each product.

----

8.   State one benefit and one limitation of using marginal, absorption or activity based costing:

	Benefit	**Limitation**
Marginal costing		
Absorption costing		
Activity based costing		

CHAPTER 12: OVERHEADS AND OVERHEAD ABSORPTION

1. Select the correct definition of an indirect cost from the following:

(a)	The cost of producing one extra unit of output.	
(b)	A cost which is shared amongst cost units, as it does not relate to one unit of output.	
(c)	The total budgeted cost of producing one unit of output.	
(d)	The total direct materials and direct labour cost of a unit of output.	

2. The following information is available about a cost centre:

	Budgeted	Actual
Overheads	£500,000	£600,000
Activity	10,000 hours	12,500 hours

The overhead absorption rate for the cost centre is:

A	£40 per hour	
B	£48 per hour	
C	£50 per hour	
D	£60 per hour	

3.   MI Ltd operates a system of absorption costing.

Canteen overhead costs are apportioned to departments on the basis of the number of employees in each department, which are:

Production   28

Assembly   52

Finance   8

Administration   12

The canteen overhead costs for the next year are forecast to be £61,000.

How much of the canteen overhead costs will be apportioned to the assembly department?

A	£17,080	
B	£21,350	
C	£31,720	
D	£39,650	

4.   The budgeted overhead and activity levels for Bedford Shoes Ltd are:

Department	Production	Packing
Budgeted overhead	£80,000	£43,200
Budgeted direct labour hours	2,500 hours	3,600 hours
Budgeted machine hours	4,000 hours	2,880 hours

Calculate the budgeted overhead absorption rates for each department on the assumption that the processes are heavily automated.

Select the two correct answers:

A	Production – £20 per hour	
B	Production – £32 per hour	
C	Packing – £12 per hour	
D	Packing – £15 per hour	

5. Overheads have been allocated and apportioned to the departments of Pentack Ltd as follows:

Department	Overhead (£)
Production 1	35,100
Production 2	26,700
Production 3	33,200
Maintenance	28,500

The maintenance department overheads are to be re-apportioned to the production departments based on the value of machinery, which is:

Department	Value of machinery (£)
Production 1	560,000
Production 2	490,000
Production 3	350,000
Total	1,400,000

The total overhead allocated to production department 2 after the maintenance department's overheads have been re-apportioned, to the nearest whole £, is:

A	£36,675	
B	£40,325	
C	£45,075	
D	£46,500	

6.   Department F3 uses machine hours to calculate the overhead absorption rate and has the following information available for the month:

Overhead absorption rate   £9.20
Actual machine hours for the month   18,375 hours
Actual overhead for the month   £167,285

(a)   Calculate the under or over absorption of overhead for the month, clearly stating if it is under or over absorbed.

(b)   Suggest an alternative overhead absorption rate department F3 could use and state the circumstances that would make it a more appropriate method.

7. Constantine Hairdressing Ltd has two revenue earning departments; hair and beauty, and one non-revenue earning department; administration.

Budgeted overheads for the next year are:

	£
Supervisor's salary – hair	35,665
Supervisor's salary – beauty	32,135
Receptionist's salary	17,500
Administration salaries	48,000
Rent and rates	50,000
Buildings insurance	15,000
Equipment depreciation	9,000
Equipment insurance	6,000
Total overheads	213,300

The following information is also available:

	Hair	Beauty	Admin.
Floor area (square metres)	240	150	110
Carrying amount of equipment	£18,000	£24,750	£2,250
Use of receptionist's time	60%	40%	–
Chargeable labour hours for the year	8,500	5,200	–

The administration department's overheads are re-apportioned to the revenue earning departments as follows:

Hair   70%

Beauty   30%

(a) Allocate and apportion the overheads to the three departments, using the table on the next page.

(b) Re-apportion the administration department's overheads to the hair and beauty departments, using the table on the next page.

(c) Calculate the overhead absorption rates for the hair and beauty departments, on the basis of chargeable labour hours for the year.

Overheads	Basis of apportionment	Total overheads	Hair	Beauty	Admin.
		£	£	£	£
Supervisor's salary – hair					
Supervisor's salary – beauty					
Receptionist's salary					
Administration salaries					
Rent and rates					
Buildings insurance					
Equipment depreciation					
Equipment insurance					
Total overheads (a)					
Re-apportion administration					
Total overheads (b)					

(c)   Overhead absorption rates:

CHAPTER 13: STANDARD COSTING AND VARIANCE ANALYSIS

Use the following information which is available about product K12 to answer questions 1 and 2:

Standard selling price per unit	£12
Budgeted sales	1,200 units
Actual sales	1,400 units
Actual sales revenue	£15,200

1.   The sales volume variance is:

A	£1,600 Adv	
B	£1,600 Fav	
C	£2,400 Adv	
D	£2,400 Fav	

2.   The sales price variance is:

A	£1,600 Adv	
B	£1,600 Fav	
C	£2,400 Adv	
D	£2,400 Fav	

Use the following information which is available about the labour costs of product S11 to answer questions 3 and 4:

Standard cost   1,000 hours at £22.00 per hour

Actual cost   1,100 hours at £21.50 per hour

3.   The labour rate variance is:

A	£550 Adv	
B	£550 Fav	
C	£2,200 Adv	
D	£2,200 Fav	

4.   The labour efficiency variance is:

A	£550 Adv	
B	£550 Fav	
C	£2,200 Adv	
D	£2,200 Fav	

5. From the explanations below, select all the ones that are correct about an adverse variance:

(a)	Actual costs are higher than standard costs.	
(b)	Actual costs are lower than standard costs.	
(c)	Actual revenue is higher than standard revenue.	
(d)	Actual revenue is lower than standard revenue.	

6. What could cause a favourable materials usage variance from the list below?

(a)	A decrease in shipping costs from materials brought in from overseas.	
(b)	A discount received from a supplier for buying in bulk.	
(c)	The use of higher skilled staff in the production line.	
(d)	Changing to a cheaper material of inferior quality.	

7. The following information is available about the material costs of product D13:

    Standard cost   580 kg at £10.50 per kg

    Actual cost   560 kg at £11.75 per kg

    Calculate the following variances and suggest possible reasons for their causes:

    (a) Materials

    (b) Materials price

    (c) Materials usage

8.   Slaveli and Co Consultants work on management projects and operate a standard costing system.

The managing partner is concerned that last month more projects were completed than anticipated, but the actual profit of £36,060 was less than the budgeted profit of £38,000.

The accountant has provided the following information for last month:

	Budget	**Actual**
Sales	80 projects at £1,200 each	90 projects at £1,150 each
Labour	10 hours per project at £35 per hour	13 hours per project at £32 per hour
Overheads	£30,000	£30,000

The accountant has also calculated the variances as follows:

Variance	**£**
Sales price	4,500 Adv
Sales volume	12,000 Fav
Labour rate	3,510 Fav
Labour efficiency	9,450 Adv

Required:

(a)   Prepare a reconciliation statement, which shows how the variances have caused the reduction in profit.

(b)   Suggest possible reasons for the variances.

CHAPTER 14: CAPITAL INVESTMENT APPRAISAL

Use the following information to answer questions 1 and 2.

Deborah Groundwork Ltd is considering investing in new machinery at a cost of £700,000 for work on a potential project. Further details about the project are:

Year	Net cash inflow/(outflow)	Discount factor
	£	at 10%
1	(100,000)	0.909
2	600,000	0.826
3	850,000	0.751
4	250,000	0.683

1.   The payback period of the project is:

A	1 year 61 days	
B	1 year 73 days	
C	2 years 86 days	
D	2 years 169 days	

2.   The net present value of the project is:

A	£513,800	
B	£818,100	
C	£900,000	
D	£1,213,800	

3.   From the statements below, select the correct definition of net present value:

(a)	The length of time it takes for the initial cost of a project to be repaid from the net cash inflows.	
(b)	The expected duration of a project.	
(c)	The total discounted cash inflows and cash outflows of a project.	
(d)	The expected rate of return of a project.	

4.   Discuss one benefit and one limitation of using the payback method in capital investment decisions.

5. Fierce Construction Ltd is considering investing in a large housing development project.

    Suggest two financial factors and two non-financial factors Fierce Construction Ltd should consider before undertaking the project.

    _____

    _____

    _____

    _____

    _____

    _____

    _____

    _____

    _____

    _____

    _____

    _____

    _____

    _____

6.   Safety Watches Ltd is considering developing an App, for which a return of 10% is required. The following information is available about the project:

	Year 0	Year 1	Year 2	Year 3	Year 4	Year 5
	£	£	£	£	£	£
Development costs	88,000	–	–	–	–	–
Sales revenue		–	76,000	160,000	174,000	204,000	54,000
Variable costs		–	38,000	80,000	87,000	102,000	27,000
Fixed costs		–	15,000	15,000	15,000	15,000	15,000
10% discount factor	1.0	0.909	0.826	0.751	0.683	0.621

(a)   Calculate the payback of the project.

(b)   Calculate the net present value of the project.

7.   The directors of Nottingsham Sports Ltd are considering two alternative investment projects. Whichever project is chosen, the company will have to borrow the initial investment at a variable interest rate of 5% per annum.

Project X involves the conversion of a local village community shop and café, which is run by volunteers, into a branded sports shop, which will be run by trained specialist staff from outside the area. The current shop is thriving, but continually makes a loss.

Project Y involves extending a sports pavilion in a deprived community. The extension will include changing and sports facilities for both women and people with disabilities, as the current pavilion only has a male changing room. The project will involve creating up to five jobs for people from the local community.

The accountant of Nottingsham Sports Ltd has carried out investment appraisals on both projects which is as follows:

	Project X	Project Y
Initial investment	£50,000	£100,000
Net present value	£70,000	£140,000
Payback period	3 years	2 years
Estimated life of the project	10 years	7 years

The net present value was calculated using a discount rate of 8% for both projects. This was based on the current return on capital employed of 3%, plus the interest rate of 5%.

Assess the two projects and recommend to the directors of Nottingsham Sports Ltd the one they should accept.

Answers

FINANCIAL ACCOUNTING
ANSWERS

CHAPTER 1: FINANCIAL STATEMENTS AND INTRODUCTION TO ETHICS

1. (a) and (d) relate to financial accounting.

    (b) and (c) relate to management accounting.

2. C

3. A

4. C

    (£11,325 − £1,065) × 5% = £513.

5.

Oliver Limited

Income Statement for the year ended 31 May 20-8

	£000	£000
Revenue		3,803
Opening inventory	75	
Purchases	2,438	
	2,513	
Less Closing inventory	79	
Cost of sales		2,434
Gross profit		1,369
Less Expenses:		
Administration expenses	485	
Distribution expenses	79	
		564
Profit for the year from operations		805
Less Finance costs		27
Profit for the year before tax		778
Less Tax		162
Profit for the year after tax		616

Statement of Changes in Equity for the year ended 31 May 20-8

	Share capital £000	Share premium £000	Retained earnings £000	Total £000
Balances at start	400	100	577	1,077
Profit for the year			616	616
Dividends paid			(236)	(236)
Balances at end	400	100	957	1,457

Statement of Financial Position as at 31 May 20-8

Non-current assets	£000 Cost	£000 Depreciation	£000 Carrying amount
Plant and equipment	2,160	757	1,403
Current assets			
Inventory		79	
Trade and other receivables		610	
Cash and cash equivalents		207	
		896	
Less Current liabilities			
Trade and other payables	215		
Tax liabilities	162		
		377	
Net Current assets			519
			1,922
Less Non-current liabilities			465
NET ASSETS			1,457
EQUITY			
Ordinary shares			400
Share premium			100
Retained earnings			957
TOTAL EQUITY			1,457

CHAPTER 2: INCOMPLETE RECORDS

1.   £19,500

(£4,000 + £15,000 + £6,500 + £3,600 – £1,400 – £8,200)

2.   B

(£16,800 + £5,100 – £9,700 = £12,200)

3.   £10,590

Dr			Bank account			Cr
20-8		£	20-8			£
31 Dec	Capital introduced	10,000	31 Dec	Trade payables		26,510
31 Dec	Trade receivables	48,900	31 Dec	Fixtures and fittings		14,000
			31 Dec	Drawings		7,800
			31 Dec	**Balance c/d**		**10,590**
		58,900				58,900
20-9			20-9			
1 Jan	Balance b/d	10,590				

4.   D

Dr			Purchases ledger control account			Cr
20-7/8		£	20-7/8			£
30 Nov	Bank payments	147,300	1 Dec	Balance b/d		13,800
30 Nov	Purchases returns	438	**30 Nov**	**Purchases (Bal.)**		**151,273**
30 Nov	Discounts received	1,685				
30 Nov	Balance c/d	15,650				
		165,073				165,073
20-8/9			20-8/9			
			1 Dec	Balance b/d		15,650

5. A

Dr			Wages account		Cr
20-7/8		£	20-7/8		£
31 Aug	**Bank payments (Bal.)**	**56,200**	1 Sep	Balance b/d	600
31 Aug	Balance c/d	900	31 Aug	Income statement	56,500
		57,100			57,100
20-8/9			20-8/9		
			1 Sep	Balance b/d	900

6. D

Dr		Disposals account		Cr
	£			£
Cost	22,000	Depreciation		14,000
Profit on sale	3,000	**Sale proceeds (Bal.)**		**11,000**
	25,000			25,000

7. £350,000

(£500,000 × (100% − 30%))

8. C

	£	£	%
Revenue		200,000	125
Opening inventory	15,000		
Purchases (Bal.)	**165,000**		
	180,000		
Less Closing inventory	(20,000)		
Cost of sales		160,000	100
Gross profit		40,000	25

9.   £750

Dr		Cash account	Cr
	£		£
Balance b/d	450	Bankings	46,200
Takings	54,600	Cash payments	7,600
		Cash Stolen (Bal.)	**750**
		Balance c/d	500
	55,050		55,050

10.   (a)   £74,418 (£14,250 – £5,600 + £56,800 + £8,968 (opening bank))

(b)   **Bernard**

Trading section of Income Statement for the year ended 31 December 20-8

	£	£
Revenue (W1)		339,018
Opening inventory	14,250	
Purchases (W2)	232,934	
	247,184	
Less Goods for own use (W4)	2,262	
	244,922	
Less Closing inventory	18,910	
Cost of sales		226,012
Gross profit (W3)		113,006

W1   Revenue £336,236 + £2,782 = £339,018

W2   Purchases

Dr	Purchases ledger control account		Cr
	£		£
Bank	225,724	Balance b/d	5,600
Bank	4,960	**Purchases (Bal.)**	**232,934**
Balance c/d	7,850		
	238,534		238,534

W3   Gross profit £339,018 × 50%/150% = £113,006

W4   Cost of sales £339,018 – £113,006 = £226,012

Goods taken for own use £226,012 + £18,910 – £232,934 – £14,250 = £2,262

(c)   **Bernard**

Income Statement for the year ended 31 December 20-8

	£	£
Gross profit		113,006
Less Expenses:		
Rent (W5)	12,000	
Loss on sale of equipment (W6)	520	
Depreciation (W7)	13,900	
General expenses	15,326	
Wages	44,000	
		85,746
Net profit for the year		27,260

W5   Rent £11,000 + £1,000 = £12,000

W6   Loss on sale of equipment

Dr	Disposals account		Cr
	£		£
Carrying value	1,200	Sale proceeds	680
		Loss on sale (Bal.)	**520**
	1,200		1,200

W7   Depreciation

Dr		Shop equipment		Cr
	£			£
Balance b/d	56,800	Disposal		1,200
		Depreciation (Bal.)		**13,900**
		Balance c/d		41,700
	56,800			56,800

(d)   **Bernard**

Statement of Financial Position as at 31 December 20-8

	£	£	£
Non-current assets			
Shop equipment			41,700
Current assets			
Inventory		18,910	
Bank (W8)		5,656	
		24,566	
Less Current liabilities			
Trade payables	7,850		
Other payables	1,000		
		8,850	
Net current assets			15,716
NET ASSETS			57,416
FINANCED BY			
Opening capital			74,418
Add Profit for the year			27,260
			101,678
Less Drawings (W9)			44,262
			57,416

W8   Bank £7,834 – £4,960 + £2,782 = £5,656

W9   Drawings £42,000 + £2,262 (goods for own use) = £44,262

CHAPTER 3: COMPUTER ACCOUNTING

1. (a), (c) and (d) are advantages.

    (b) is a disadvantage.

2. The costs that could be incurred include:

    • the initial capital cost of the hardware and software, including installation costs

    • ongoing costs relating to software, such as replacements, updating and support

    • costs associated with disruption while the new system is installed, this may include staff overtime and IT specialists and the costs of running both the old and new systems for a period of time

    • staff training costs

    • there may be staff redundancies

    • back up and security, the costs associated with ensuring that data is backed up and secure at all times.

3. Disadvantages include any two from the following list:

Disadvantages	Explanation
cost	the capital costs of hardware and software and the costs of training, maintenance and updating
staff opposition	some employees may not like computers and some jobs may be lost as manual processes are automated
system failure	if software crashes or hardware fails, there will be disruption to the workflow and in a worst-case scenario, loss of data which may not have been backed up
errors	although data entry is made simpler with a computer based system, errors can still occur and go undetected

security	there is always the danger of the system being hacked, viruses entering a system and risk of data theft by staff
health and safety	the increasing use of computers at work may aggravate the problems of bad backs, eyestrain and muscular complaints

4. **Benefits** of spreadsheets include:

- **speed**

  the use of formulae enables figures to be changed and the results seen immediately

- **ease of use**

  a correctly set up spreadsheet will allow users to input data easily

- **output**

  printouts and reports can be produced easily.

  Drawbacks of spreadsheets include:

- **inaccurate information**

  formulae may be set up incorrectly, therefore the information produced may be inaccurate

- **security**

  if passwords and restricted access to use are not in place, data may be accidentally or intentionally altered

- **corruption**

  data may become corrupted and therefore potentially lost

- **back up**

  correct back up procedures must be in place, there is a danger of a spreadsheet being out of date or two users using different versions of the same file.

CHAPTER 4: PARTNERSHIP FINANCIAL STATEMENTS

1.   (a), (b) and (c) are false.

   (d) is true.

2.   B

   $((£12,000 \times 5\%) + £53,400) \div 2 = £27,000$

3.   A

Dr		Current account – Margaret		Cr
	£			£
Drawings	15,000	Salary		16,000
Interest on drawings	300	Interest on capital		2,250
Balance c/d (Bal.)	**21,950**	Share of profit		19,000
	37,250			37,250

4.

Alison, Bernadette and Coleen

Profit appropriation account for the year ended 31 March 20-8

	£	£
Profit for the year		66,500
Less appropriation of profit:		
Salary:		
Alison	10,000	
Coleen	20,000	
	———	
		30,000
Interest on capital:		
Alison (£10,000 × 3%)	300	
Bernadette (£30,000 × 3%)	900	
Coleen (£10,000 × 3%)	300	
	———	
		1,500
		———
		35,000
		———
Share of remaining profit		
Alison (£35,000 × 30%)	10,500	
Bernadette (£35,000 × 50%)	17,500	
Coleen (£35,000 × 20%)	7,000	
	———	
		35,000
		———

5.

Dr					Capital accounts				Cr
20-8		Eliza	Sam	20-8			Eliza	Sam
		£	£				£	£
				1 Jan	Balance b/d		40,000	30,000
31 Dec	Balance c/d	40,000	30,000					
		40,000	30,000				40,000	30,000
20-9				20-9				
				1 Jan	Balance b/d		40,000	30,000

Dr				Current accounts			Cr	
20-8		Eliza	Sam	20-8			Eliza	Sam
		£	£				£	£
1 Jan	Balance b/d	480		1 Jan	Balance b/d			1,310
31 Dec	Drawings	12,000	28,640	31 Dec	Salary		8,000	
31 Dec	Interest on drawings	600	1,432	31 Dec	Interest on capital		2,400	1,800
				31 Dec	Share of profit (W1)		18,660	12,440
31 Dec	Balance c/d	15,980		31 Dec	Balance c/d			14,522
		29,060	30,072				29,060	30,072
20-9				20-9				
1 Jan	Balance b/d		14,522	1 Jan	Balance b/d		15,980	

W1   Share of profit £41,268 + £600 + £1,432 − £8,000 − £2,400 − £1,800 = £31,100

Eliza £31,100 × 60% = £18,660, Sam £31,100 × 40% = £12,440

6.   **Obscure Fiction partnership**

Income Statement for the year ended 31 March 20-8

	£	£
Revenue		79,800
Opening inventory	5,865	
Purchases	36,750	
	42,615	
Less Closing inventory	6,273	
Cost of sales		36,342
Gross profit		43,458
Add: Discounts received		524
Less Expenses:		
Wages (W1)	7,436	
Rent and rates (W2)	7,800	
Sundry expenses	585	
Credit card charges	880	
Motor expenses	689	
Depreciation (W3)	6,200	
		23,590
Profit for the year		20,392

W1   Wages £7,380 + £56 = £7,436

W2   Rent and rates £8,300 − £500 = £7,800

W3   Depreciation £24,800 × 25% = £6,200

Dr   **Capital accounts**   **Cr**

20-7/8		Ayesha	Josh	20-7/8		Ayesha	Josh
		£	£			£	£
				1 Apr	Balance b/d	25,000	25,000
31 Mar	Balance c/d	25,000	25,000				
		25,000	25,000			25,000	25,000
20-8				20-8			
				1 Apr	Balance b/d	25,000	25,000

Dr   **Current accounts**   **Cr**

20-7/8		Ayesha	Josh	20-7/8		Ayesha	Josh
		£	£			£	£
1 Apr	Balance b/d	450		1 Apr	Balance b/d		180
31 Mar	Drawings	6,845	13,050	31 Mar	Salary		6,000
				31 Mar	Interest on capital (W4)	1,250	1,250
				31 Mar	Share of profit (W5)	5,946	5,946
31 Mar	Balance c/d		326	31 Mar	Balance c/d	99	
		7,295	13,376			7,295	13,376
20-8				20-8			
1 Apr	Balance b/d	99		1 Apr	Balance b/d		326

W4   Interest on capital £25,000 × 5% = £1,250 each

W5   Share of profit £20,392 − £6,000 − £1,250 − £1,250 = £11,892 ÷ 2 = £5,946

Obscure Fiction partnership

Statement of Financial Position as at 31 March 20-8

Non-current assets	£ Cost	£ Depreciation	£ Carrying amount
Equipment	24,800	6,200	18,600
Current assets			
Inventory		6,273	
Other receivables		500	
Bank		27,800	
		34,573	
Less Current liabilities			
Trade payables	2,890		
Other payables	56		
		2,946	
Net current assets			31,627
NET ASSETS			50,227
FINANCED BY:			
Capital accounts:			
Ayesha			25,000
Josh			25,000
			50,000
Current accounts:			
Ayesha		(99)	
Josh		326	227
TOTAL EQUITY			50,227

CHAPTER 5: CHANGES IN PARTNERSHIPS

1. (c)

2. D

    Dr Goodwill, Cr Capital accounts (old profit sharing ratio), Clive is £10,000 (£50,000 × 20%)

    Cr Goodwill, Dr Capital accounts (new profit sharing ratio), Clive is £20,000 (£50,000 × 40%)

3. **B**

Dr		Capital account – Donald		Cr
	£			£
Bank	50,000	Balance b/d		30,000
Loan (Bal.)	**25,000**	Share of goodwill		45,000
	75,000			75,000

4.

Dr				Capital accounts			Cr
	D	E	F		D	E	F
	£		£		£		£
Share of goodwill	38,400	12,800	12,800	Balance b/d	30,000	30,000	
				Bank			50,000
				Share of goodwill	32,000	32,000	
Balance c/d	31,400	57,000	37,200	Reval.	7,800	7,800	
	69,800	69,800	50,000		69,800	69,800	50,000
				Balance b/d	31,400	57,000	37,200

5.   **'IT for Novices'**

Partnership appropriation account for the year ended 31 December 20-8

	Three months ended 31 March 20-8 £	Nine months ended 31 December 20-8 £	Total £
Profit for the year	30,000	90,000	120,000
Less appropriation of profit:			
Salary:			
Xaviar	4,500	13,500	18,000
Yan	6,000	18,000	24,000
Zain	0	9,000	9,000
	10,500	40,500	51,000
Interest on capital:			
Xaviar	240	720	960
Yan	210	630	840
Zain	0	450	450
	450	1,800	2,250
Remaining profit	19,050	47,700	66,750
Share of remaining profit:			
Xaviar	13,335	28,620	41,955
Yan	5,715	9,540	15,255
Zain	0	9,540	9,540
	19,050	47,700	66,750

6. **'Our Local Café' partnership**

Income Statement for the year ended 31 December 20-8

	£	£
Revenue		266,700
Opening inventory	10,200	
Purchases	151,438	
	161,638	
Less Goods for own use	750	
	160,888	
Less Closing inventory	15,300	
Cost of sales		145,588
Gross profit		121,112
Less Expenses:		
Wages	29,200	
Office costs	10,196	
Sundry expenses	1,386	
		40,782
Profit for the year		80,330

Share of profit:

Peggy (£80,330 × 40%)	32,132
Nora (£80,330 × 40%)	32,132
Queenie (£80,330 × 20%)	16,066
	80,330

Capital accounts

Dr							Cr			
20-8		Peggy £	Nora £	Queenie £		20-8		Peggy £	Nora £	Queenie £
1 Jan	Goodwill	26,000	26,000	13,000		1 Jan	Balance b/d	15,000	15,000	
						1 Jan	Bank			44,500
						1 Jan	Revaluation	10,000	10,000	
31 Dec	Balance c/d	31,500	31,500	31,500		1 Jan	Goodwill	32,500	32,500	
		57,500	57,500	44,500				57,500	57,500	44,500
20-9						20-9				
						1 Jan	Balance b/d	31,500	31,500	31,500

Current accounts

Dr							Cr			
20-8		Peggy £	Nora £	Queenie £		20-8		Peggy £	Nora £	Queenie £
31 Dec	Drawings	33,000	32,000	17,000		1 Jan	Balance b/d	580	630	
31 Dec	Own use	750				31 Dec	Profit	32,132	32,132	16,066
31 Dec	Balance c/d		762			31 Dec	Balance c/d	1,038		934
		33,750	32,762	17,000				33,750	32,762	17,000
20-9						20-9				
1 Jan	Balance b/d	1,038		934		1 Jan	Balance b/d		762	

'Our Local Café' partnership

Statement of Financial Position as at 31 December 20-8

	£	£	£
Non-current assets			
Property			50,000
Current assets			
Inventory		15,300	
Bank		43,550	
		_____	
		58,850	
Less Current liabilities			
Trade payables	15,560		
	_____		
		15,560	
		_____	
Net current assets			43,290
			_____
NET ASSETS			93,290
			_____
FINANCED BY:			
Capital accounts:			
Peggy			31,500
Nora			31,500
Queenie			31,500
			_____
			94,500
Current accounts:			
Peggy		(1,038)	
Nora		762	
Queenie		(934)	(1,210)
		_____	_____
TOTAL EQUITY			93,290
			_____

CHAPTER 6: ACCOUNTING FOR LIMITED COMPANIES

1.   (a), (b), (d), (f) and (h) are true.

      (c), (e) and (g) are false.

2.   (d)

3.   (a), (b) and (c) are false.

      (d) is true.

4.   (a)   The responsibilities of directors under the Companies Act 2006 are to:

   - act within their powers in accordance with the company's constitution

   - promote the company's success

   - act independently

   - ensure they take reasonable care and due diligence

   - ensure they have the correct skills

   - avoid conflicts of interest

   - not accept benefits from third parties

   - disclose interests in any proposed transactions involving the company

   - ensure the accounting records and financial statements are properly maintained.

(b) The items which should be contained within the directors' report include:

- the principle activities of the company

- a review of the activities over the last year

- likely future developments that will affect the company

- the names of the directors and their shareholdings

- significant differences in property valuations (book value compared to market value)

- political and charitable donations

- actions taken on employee involvement and consultation

- the company policy on the employment of disabled people

- the company policy on health and safety

- the company policy on the payment of suppliers

5. External stakeholders and their interests include any two from the following:

customers   to ensure goods and services will be available in the future

suppliers   to ensure the company can pay for goods and services supplied

lenders   to view the security available on loans and the company's ability to pay its commitments

government   to ensure taxes are paid and business statistics are collated

local community   to view the contribution the company makes to the economy

Internal stakeholders and their interests include any two from the following:

shareholders   to establish the company's profitability and the dividends paid

management   to see the future prospects of the company

employees   to ensure the company's ability to pay and future employment

6. Benefits of published accounts include any two from the following:

produced annually	reports can be reviewed at least once a year and comparisons made
available to all shareholders	the financial statements must be made available to all shareholders; therefore, performance can be reviewed
filed with Companies House	for private companies the filing deadline is nine months and public companies the filing deadline is six months, this means companies have a time limit for producing the required information
larger companies require an audit	an independent audit is a requirement for larger companies which means that the contents are verified by someone outside of the company
prepared in accordance with the accounting framework	the same legal and accounting standards are followed, which enable comparisons to be made

Limitations of published accounts include any two from the following:

information is out of date	the information is historic and does not show any recent changes that may have occurred
additional information is not disclosed	only the information required by the accounting framework will be included
information gives no indication of future performance	the information gives little indication of what may happen in the future
information is financial only	the information is limited to financial performance only, there is no indication of non-financial performance, such as customer satisfaction or quality control

7.   B

   200,000 × 4 = 800,000 shares, ÷ 8 = 100,000 new shares, × 50p = £50,000.

   Note: The shares are 25p shares, therefore multiply by 4.

8.   **Georgie Ltd**

   Statement of Changes in Equity for the year ended 31 December 20-8

	Share capital £000	Share premium £000	Retained earnings £000	Reval. reserve £000	Total £000
At 1 January 20-8	300	50	41	–	391
Issue of shares (W1)	60	(50)	(10)	–	–
Revaluation	–	–	–	200	200
Profit for the year	–	–	285	–	285
Dividends paid	–	–	(240)	–	(240)
At 31 December 20-8	360	–	76	200	636

   W1   Bonus issue £300,000 × 10 (10p shares) = 3,000,000 shares ÷ 5 = 600,000 × 10p = £60,000.

   The bonus shares have been issued from the share premium account first, and the remainder from retained earnings.

   Note: Only dividends paid are included.

9.   **Fitness plc**

Non-current assets note for the year ended 31 May 20-8

	Land and buildings £000	Plant and equipment £000	Total £000
Cost			
At 1 June 20-7	250	425	675
Additions at cost	–	162	162
Less Cost of disposals	–	(40)	(40)
Revaluation	100	–	100
At 31 May 20-8	**350**	**547**	**897**
Depreciation			
At 1 June 20-7	25	237	262
Charge for the year (W1)	7	80	87
Less Eliminated on disposal	–	(10)	(10)
Less Eliminated on revaluation	(25)	–	(25)
At 31 May 20-8	**7**	**307**	**314**
Carrying amount at 31 May 20-8	**343**	**240**	**583**

W1   Depreciation land and buildings £350,000 × 2% = £7,000

Depreciation plant and equipment (£425,000 + £162,000 − £40,000 − £237,000 + £10,000) × 25% = £80,000

10. **Victor Ltd**

Income Statement for the year ended 31 March 20-8

	£000	£000
Revenue		1,084
Opening inventory	57	
Purchases	484	
	541	
Less Closing inventory	65	
Cost of sales		476
Gross profit		608
Less Expenses:		
Administration expenses (W1)	223	
Distribution expenses (W2)	197	
	420	
Profit for the year from operations		188
Less Finance costs		2
Profit for the year before tax		186
Less Tax		35
Profit for the year after tax		151

W1   Administration expenses

	£000	
Per trial balance	131	
Irrecoverable debts	17	
Depreciation	75	£750,000 × 20% × 50%
	223	

W2   Distribution expenses

	£000	
Per trial balance	122	
Depreciation	75	£750,000 × 20% × 50%
	197	

Victor Ltd

Statement of Changes in Equity for the year ended 31 March 20-8

	Share capital £000	Share premium £000	Retained earnings £000	Reval. reserve £000	Total £000
At 1 April 20-7	300	150	107	–	557
Revaluation	–	–	–	70	70
Profit for the year	–	–	151	–	151
Dividends paid	–	–	(136)	–	(136)
At 31 March 20-8	300	150	122	70	642

Victor Ltd

Statement of Financial Position as at 31 March 20-8

	£000 Cost/ Valuation	£000 Depreciation	£000 Carrying amount
Non-current assets			
Property	450	–	450
Plant and equipment (W3)	750	635	115
	1,200	635	565
Current assets			
Inventory		65	
Trade receivables (W4)		177	
		242	
Less Current liabilities			
Bank overdraft	48		
Trade payables	82		
Tax liabilities	35		
		165	
Net current assets			77
NET ASSETS			642
EQUITY			
Ordinary shares			300
Share premium			150
Retained earnings			122
Revaluation reserve			70
TOTAL EQUITY			642

W3   Depreciation plant and equipment £485,000 + £150,000 = £635,000

W4   Trade receivables £194,000 – £17,000 = £177,000

CHAPTER 7: STATEMENT OF CASH FLOWS

1. (c)

2. D

	£
Loss from operations	(6,846)
Depreciation	5,064
Loss on sale of non-current assets	782
Decrease in inventory	2,889
Increase in trade receivables	(3,015)
Increase in trade payables	2,930
Cash from operating activities	**1,804**

3. D

£5,127 + £9,084 = £14,211.

Note: The change in the bank loan is included in financing activities.

4. A

	£
Proceeds from the sale of non-current assets	8,500
Purchase of non-current assets	(86,000)
Dividends received	1,200
Investing activities	**(76,300)**

5.   C

	£
Receipts from the issue of share capital	10,250
Increase in non-current loans	6,000
Dividends paid	(15,000)
	————
Financing activities	**1,250**
	————

6.

Purchase of non-current assets = £14,942:

Dr		Property, plant and equipment		Cr
	£			£
Balance b/d	57,248	Depreciation		7,283
Additions (Bal.)	**14,942**	Disposal		1,800
		Balance c/d		63,107
	72,190			72,190

Proceeds from the sale of non-current assets = £2,050:

Dr		Disposals		Cr
	£			£
Property, plant and equip.	1,800	Sale proceeds (Bal.)		**2,050**
Profit on sale	250			
	2,050			2,050

7. **Ninety Ltd**

Statement of Cash Flows for the year ended 31 December 20-8

	£000	£000
Profit from operations (W1)		1,805
Depreciation		276
Profit on sale of non-current assets (W3)		(3)
Decrease in inventory		11
Increase in trade receivables		(32)
Increase in trade payables		16
Cash from operating activities		**2,073**
Interest paid		(152)
Tax paid		(353)
Net cash from operating activities		**1,568**
Investing activities		
Purchase of non-current assets	(784)	
Proceeds from sale of non-current assets	14	
Net cash used in investing activities		**(770)**
Financing activities		
Receipts from issue of share capital (W4)	230	
Increase in non-current loans	315	
Dividends paid	(1,386)	
Net cash used in financing activities		**(841)**
Net decrease in cash and cash equivalents		**(43)**
Cash and cash equivalents at the start of the year		107
Cash and cash equivalents at the end of the year		64

W1   Profit from operations

	£000
Decrease in retained earnings:	
Retained earnings at 31 December 20-8	4,162
Less Retained earnings at 31 December 20-7	4,275
	(113)
Add back:	
Dividends paid	1,386
Tax provision	380
Finance costs	152
Profit from operations	1,805

W2   Cost of non-current assets sold

	£000
Cost at 31 December 20-8	8,570
Less Additions	784
	7,786
Less Cost at 31 December 20-7	7,825
Cost of non-current assets sold	(39)

W3   Profit on disposal of non-current assets

	£000
Cost of non-current assets sold (W2)	39
Less Depreciation	(28)
	11
Less Sale proceeds	(14)
Profit on disposal	(3)

W4   Receipts from issue of share capital

		£000
Increase in share capital:		
Ordinary shares at 31 December 20-8		1,700
Share premium at 31 December 20-8		280
		1,980
Less		
Ordinary shares at 31 December 20-7	1,500	
Share premium at 31 December 20-7	250	1,750
Issue of share capital		230

CHAPTER 8: INTERPRETATION OF ACCOUNTING INFORMATION

1. A

Dividend yield = dividend per share ÷ market price per share × 100

Dividend per share = £360,000 ÷ 300,000 = £1.20

Dividend yield = £1.20 ÷ £4.80 × 100 = 25%

2. B

Earnings per share = profit after tax ÷ number of issued shares

= £450,000 ÷ 300,000 = £1.50

3. **A**

Dividend cover = profit after tax ÷ ordinary share dividends paid

= £450,000 ÷ £360,000 = 1.25 times

4. B

Price earnings = current market price per share ÷ earnings per share

= £4.80 ÷ £1.50 (see answer 2) = 3.20

5. D

Interest cover = profit before interest and tax ÷ interest payable

= £630,000 ÷ £20,000 = 31.50 times

6. (c)

7. Limitations of financial ratios to make an investment decision include:

- the calculations are based on information which is historic, they do not reflect what the state of the companies are at present or in the future.

- the financial statements of the two companies may have been prepared using different accounting policies, such as the depreciation policy, this may make comparisons difficult.

- the impact of inflation is not usually taken into account in the preparation of financial statements and most items are recorded at their original cost, so this could distort comparisons.

- a 'poor' ratio does not necessarily mean poor performance, a company may have been operating successfully with similar ratios for a long time, therefore ratios should be considered alongside other available information.

8.

Ratio	30 April 20-8	Workings
Gross profit margin	26%	£2,808,000 ÷ £10,800,000 × 100 = 26%
Profit in relation to revenue	12%	£1,296,000 ÷ £10,800,000 × 100 = 12%
Return on capital employed	80.15%	£1,486,000 ÷ (£1,356,000 + £498,000) × 100 = 80.15%
Interest cover	7.82 times	£1,486,000 ÷ £190,000 = 7.82 times
Current ratio	1.30 : 1	£3,504,000 ÷ £2,700,000 = 1.30 : 1
Liquid capital ratio	1.06 : 1	(£3,504,000 - £654,000) ÷ £2,700,000 = 1.06 : 1
Trade receivables days	96.32 days	£2,850,000 ÷ £10,800,000 × 365 = 96.32 days
Trade payable days	79.90 days	£1,750,000 ÷ £7,994,000 × 365 = 79.90 days
Rate of inventory turnover days	29.82 days	(£652,000 + £654,000) ÷ 2 ÷ £7,992,000 × 365 = 29.82 days
Capital gearing	26.86%	£498,000 ÷ (£498,000 + £1,356,000) × 100 = 26.86%

9.

REPORT
To: Mike
From: AQA accounting student
Subject: Potential investment in Calvin Ltd
Date: Today

I have reviewed the financial statements and ratios for Calvin Ltd and identified the following:

Profitability

The gross profit and profit from operations have both increased, however, there has been a decline in both the gross profit margin (35% to 26%) and the profit in relation to revenue (19% to 12%).

The decrease in gross profit margin is probably due to a decrease in selling price, as sales have almost doubled, and this would suggest a greater volume of sales than in the previous year, it could indicate that the company is growing too rapidly, which could be worrying. However, overhead control would appear to be good as the percentage fall in the profit relation to revenue is lower than the fall in the gross profit margin.

The return on capital employed has more than doubled which is a good sign, however, it is largely due to the decrease in the capital employed.

The finance costs have increased vastly, and interest cover has fallen from over 60 times, to just below eight times. The increased finance costs appear to have been due to the use of a bank overdraft as opposed to a long-term loan in the previous year, which indicates the company is riskier than it was previously.

Liquidity

Both the current and liquid capital ratios have fallen, which is a cause for concern.

Although inventory has remained constant, there has been a big increase in both trade receivables and trade payables, and the company has moved from money in the bank to a large overdraft.

Efficiency

Trade receivables days have increased by approximately 34 days, which means customers are taking longer to pay. This may be due to offering customers extended credit periods to encourage them to buy more.

Trade payable days have also increased by around 40 days, this indicates that the company is struggling to pay its debts on time, which could be due to customers taking longer to pay.

The rate of inventory turnover has fallen by approximately 20 days, this could mean that the company is struggling to pay for inventory, or the increase in sales has meant that it is being used more quickly than previously. If inventory levels become too low, there may be insufficient levels to meet future demand.

Capital structure

A comparison of the gearing shows that there has been a slight improvement from 28.33% to 26.86%, this means that less reliance is placed on the banks for long-term funding.

However, the increase in the bank overdraft and finance costs may indicate that banks are no longer willing to lend the company money, this makes the company much riskier.

Conclusion

I do not recommend that you invest in Calvin Ltd at this point in time, it may be worth seeking some further information from the company about its current financial position.

Note: In a question of this nature, make sure you are able to back up your decision with valid points.

10.

Differences between the profit from operations and the fall in the bank balance are due to:

- profit from operations is the surplus of income over expenditure for the financial period and adjustments are made for accruals, prepayments and non-cash items (such as depreciation)

- the bank balance is what the company physically has in cash at the end of the year, in this case it is overdrawn and therefore owes money to the bank.

The statement of cash flows shows the cash which has gone in and out of the company in the last year; explanations of the figures for Turkish Baths plc are:

Cash from operating activities

In this section depreciation of £516,000 has been added back to profit, as it is a non-cash item.

Inventory has increased by £502,000, which suggests that the company has bought more, and cash has decreased.

Trade receivables have also increased by £368,000. This would indicate that revenue is higher, or credit control processes are not working effectively, and cash has decreased.

There is an increase in trade payables, but the amount is not as significant as the increase in inventory. This increases the cash by £31,000.

Net cash from operating activities

The profit from operations does not reflect the interest and tax payments which have been paid out of the bank, totalling £771,000.

Investing activities

The purchase of non-current assets is not reflected in the profit from operations and cash has decreased by £2,584,000 from investing in them.

Financing activities

There has been a decrease in the non-current loan of £580,000, which is not included in profit from operations.

Dividends paid to shareholders total £334,000. These are not included in profit from operations.

Both figures reduce the amount of cash.

CHAPTER 9: ACCOUNTING REGULATIONS AND ETHICS

1.   (a), (b) and (d) are true.

    (c) is false.

2.   B

3.   C

4.   B

5.   C

6.   Safeguards include any three from:

    - corporate governance regulations

    - education and training requirements from professional bodies

    - continuing professional development

    - relevant experience

    - external review of work

    - professional and regulatory monitoring

    - adherence to professional standards

    - disciplinary procedures

    - policies and procedures to ensure compliance.

        Note: The list is not exhaustive and other points may be valid.

7. Corporate Social Responsibility policies include any two from:

- using local or ethical suppliers

- running fuel efficient vehicles

- setting recycling targets

- encouraging employees to carry out voluntary activities for the local community or charities

- allowing flexible working arrangements for employees.

    Note: The list is not exhaustive and other examples may be valid.

8. An accountant in practice should:

- establish the facts

- determine whether the acts are unethical or illegal

- seek external advice if required, from their professional body or a legal advisor

- consider ceasing to work for the client

- if the law has been broken, the accountant may have an obligation to report it to the relevant authority.

    Note: The list is not exhaustive and other steps may be valid.

MANAGEMENT ACCOUNTING
ANSWERS

CHAPTER 10: MANAGEMENT ACCOUNTING: THE USE OF BUDGETS

1.   (b), (c) and (d) relate to management accounting.

(a) relates to financial accounting.

2.   (c)

3.   D

Closing inventory is 1,965 units (7,860 × 25%).

Production budget = 6,240 − 1,560 + 1,965 = 6,645 units.

4.   B

	£	
July purchases	10,500	(£21,000 × 50%)
August purchases	11,500	(£23,000 × 50%)
Less August cash discount	(230)	(£11,500 × 2%)
	21,770	

5.   50 hours shortfall

	Hours	
Hours required	1,050	(3.5 × 300)
Hours available	(1,000)	
Shortfall	50	

6.

	Jan	Feb	Mar	Apr
Units	800	880	880	836
	£	£	£	£
Sales (units × £15.50)	12,400	13,640	13,640	12,958

	May	Jun	Total
Units	800	920	5,116
	£	£	£
Sales (units × £15.50)	12,400	14,260	79,298

Workings:

February and March	800 units × 1.1 = 880 units
April	880 units × 0.95 = 836 units
June	800 units × 1.15 = 920 units

7.

	Month 1	Month 2	Month 3	Month 4
Production budget	Units	Units	Units	Units
Sales	500	600	560	650
Opening inventory	(125)	(150)	(140)	(160)
Closing inventory (W1)	150	140	160	150
Production	**525**	**590**	**580**	**640**
Purchases budget	kg	kg	kg	kg
Production (× 3)	1,575	1,770	1,740	1,920
Opening inventory	(315)	(354)	(348)	(384)
Closing inventory (W2)	354	348	384	366
Purchases	**1,614**	**1,764**	**1,776**	**1,902**
Purchases budget	£	£	£	£
Purchases (× £0.50)	**807**	**882**	**888**	**951**

W1   Closing inventory (finished units)

Month 1	600 × 25% = 150
Month 2	560 × 25% = 140
Month 3	650 × 25% = 162.5, but cannot exceed 160
Month 4	600 × 25% = 150

W2   Closing inventory (materials)

Month 1	1,770 ÷ 5 = 354
Month 2	1,740 ÷ 5 = 348
Month 3	1,920 ÷ 5 = 384
Month 4	1,830 ÷ 5 = 366

8.

	April	May	June
Receipts:	£	£	£
Month of sale (W1)	12,000	15,000	18,000
Less Discount (W2)	(360)	(450)	(540)
Month after sale (W3)	16,800	18,000	22,500
Less Irrecoverable debts (W4)	(840)	(900)	(1,125)
Total	**27,600**	**31,650**	**38,835**

W1   Month of sale

  April   £30,000 × 40% = £12,000

  May   £37,500 × 40% = £15,000

  June   £45,000 × 40% = £18,000

W2   Discount

  April   £12,000 × 3% = £360

  May   £15,000 × 3% = £450

  June   £18,000 × 3% = £540

W3   Month after sale

  April   £16,800

  May   £30,000 × 60% = £18,000

  June   £37,500 × 60% = £22,500

W4   Irrecoverable debts

  April   £16,800 × 5% = £840

  May   £18,000 × 5% = £900

  June   £22,500 × 5% = £1,125

9.

(a)   **Cash budget for 'The IT Shop' for the period ended 31 March 20-8:**

	January	February	March
	£	£	£
Receipts:			
Cash sales	1,500	1,600	1,650
Credit sales (W1)	18,293	21,284	24,066
Total receipts	**19,793**	**22,884**	**25,716**
Payments:			
Purchases	4,250	5,750	6,000
Shop refit	–	28,000	–
Operating expenses	3,600	3,600	3,600
Drawings	1,800	1,800	1,800
Total payments	**9,650**	**39,150**	**11,400**
Net cash flow	**10,143**	**(16,266)**	**14,316**
Opening bank/(overdraft)	**5,866**	**16,009**	**(257)**
Closing bank/(overdraft)	**16,009**	**(257)**	**14,059**

W1   Credit sales

Month of sale:	Jan (£)	Feb (£)	Mar (£)	Notes
Nov	4,800	–	–	
Dec	6,800	5,100	–	F £11,900 – £6,800
Jan	6,900	9,200	6,900	J £23,000 × 30% F £23,000 × 40% M £23,000 × 30%
Discount Jan	(207)	–	–	£6,900 × 3%
Feb	–	7,200	9,600	F £24,000 × 30% M £24,000 × 40%
Discount Feb	–	(216)	–	£7,200 × 3%
Mar	–	–	7,800	M £26,000 × 30%
Discount Mar	–	–	(234)	£7,800 × 3%
Total	**18,293**	**21,284**	**24,066**	

(b)   Increase in overdraft:

- based on the figures in the cash budget the bank will be overdrawn in February only, by £257

- this figure is within the overdraft limit of £1,000

- if sales do not reach the forecast or the shop refit cost is higher than anticipated, it may be advisable to ask for a temporary higher increase in the limit.

10.   **'The IT Shop'**

Budgeted Income Statement for the period ended 31 March 20-8

	£	£
Revenue (W1)		77,750
Opening inventory	1,684	
Purchases (W2)	18,250	
	19,934	
Less Closing inventory	2,400	
Cost of sales		17,534
Gross profit		60,216
Less Expenses:		
Discounts allowed (W3)	657	
Operating expenses (W4)	10,800	
Depreciation	1,500	
		12,957
Net profit for the period		47,259

W1   Revenue

	£	
Jan	24,500	(£1,500 + £23,000)
Feb	25,600	(£1,600 + £24,000)
Mar	27,650	(£1,650 + £26,000)
	77,750	

W2   Purchases

	£
Jan	5,750
Feb	6,000
Mar	6,500
	18,250

W3   Discounts allowed

	£
Jan	207
Feb	216
Mar	234
	657

W4   Operating expenses

	£
Jan	3,600
Feb	3,600
Mar	3,600
	10,800

'The IT Shop'

Budgeted Statement of Financial Position as at 31 March 20-8

	£	£	£
Non-current assets			
Carrying value (W5)			31,500
Current assets			
Inventory		2,400	
Trade receivables (W6)		25,400	
Bank		14,059	
		41,859	
Less Current liabilities			
Trade payables	6,500		
		6,500	
Net current assets			35,359
NET ASSETS			66,859
FINANCED BY			
Opening capital			25,000
Add Profit for the period			47,259
			72,259
Less Drawings (W7)			5,400
			66,859

W5   Non-current assets

	£
At 1 January 20-8	5,000
Shop refit	28,000
Less Depreciation	(1,500)
	31,500

W6   Trade receivables

	£	
Feb	7,200	(£24,000 × 30%)
Mar	18,200	(£26,000 × 70%)
	25,400	

W7   Drawings

	£
Jan	1,800
Feb	1,800
Mar	1,800
	5,400

CHAPTER 11: ABSORPTION AND ACTIVITY BASED COSTING

1. (c)

2. (a) relates to activity based costing.

    (b) and (d) relate to marginal costing.

    (c) relates to absorption costing.

3. D

    (£450 + £510 + £480) ÷ 150 = £9.60 per unit

4. A

    £2.25 + £1.50 = £3.75 per unit

5. D

    (£22,000 + £88,000) ÷ (£100 − £45) = 2,000 units

6. C

    (£360 + £40) × 1.25 = £500

7.

	Honey Dew	Sunflower
	£	£
Direct materials (W1)	29,600	51,000
Direct labour (W2)	7,200	21,600
Total direct cost	36,800	72,600
Overheads:		
Machinery set-ups (W3)	13,200	52,800
Quality inspections (W4)	2,000	12,000
Total cost	52,000	137,400
Total cost per unit (W5)	**13.00**	**22.90**
Selling price per unit	18.00	22.50
Profit/(loss) per unit	**5.00**	**(0.40)**

W1   Direct materials

     Honey Dew   £7.40 × 4,000 = £29,600

     Sunflower   £8.50 × 6,000 = £51,000

W2   Direct labour

     Honey Dew   £1.80 × 4,000 = £7,200

     Sunflower   £3.60 × 6,000 = £21,600

W3   Machinery set-ups

				£
Honey Dew	4,000 × 3 set-ups	12,000	× £1.10	13,200
Sunflower	6,000 × 8 set-ups	48,000	× £1.10	52,800
Total set-ups		60,000		66,000
Cost per set-up	£66,000 ÷ 60,000	£1.10		

W4   Quality inspections

				£
Honey Dew	4,000 × 1 inspection	4,000	× £0.50	2,000
Sunflower	6,000 × 4 inspections	24,000	× £0.50	12,000
Total inspections		28,000		14,000

Cost per inspection   £14,000 ÷ 28,000   £0.50

W5   Total cost per unit

Honey Dew   £52,000 ÷ 4,000 = £13.00

Sunflower   £137,400 ÷ 6,000 = £22.90

8.   Any one benefit and one limitation for each from the following:

	Benefit	**Limitation**
Marginal costing	Simple to calculate and understand	Not acceptable under IAS 2
	Can assist with make or buy decisions	Cost per unit does not include any overhead, therefore selling price is less accurate
Absorption costing	Acceptable under IAS 2	Not useful for short term decision making
	Cost per unit includes overhead absorbed using labour or machine hours, which is fine for traditional businesses	Less accurate method of establishing selling price where complex overheads are involved
Activity based costing	Acceptable under IAS 2	Time consuming to set-up and record
	Uses activities to absorb overheads, which should make the calculation of the selling price more accurate	Selecting cost drivers can be difficult

CHAPTER 12: OVERHEADS AND OVERHEAD ABSORPTION

1. (b)

2. C

    £500,000 ÷ 10,000 = £50

3. C

    £61,000 ÷ 100 × 52 = £31,720

4. A and D

    Production £80,000 ÷ 4,000 = £20 per hour

    Packing £43,200 ÷ 2,880 = £15 per hour

5. A

    (£28,500 ÷ 1,400,000 × 490,000) + £26,700 = £36,675

6.   (a)   £1,765 over absorbed

		£
Overhead absorbed	18,375 × £9.20	169,050
Actual overhead		167,285
Over absorbed		1,765

   (b)   An alternative method is labour hours.

The overhead is absorbed on the basis of the number of direct labour hours worked.

This method would be more appropriate for a department which is very labour intensive and has a high proportion of overhead incurred from labour related activities, rather than machine-based activities.

7. (a) and (b)

Overheads	Basis of apportionment	Total overheads	Hair	Beauty	Admin.
		£	£	£	£
Supervisor's salary – hair	Allocated	35,665	35,665	–	–
Supervisor's salary – beauty	Allocated	32,135	–	32,135	–
Receptionist's salary (W1)	Use of receptionist's time	17,500	10,500	7,000	–
Administration salaries	Allocated	48,000	–	–	48,000
Rent and rates (W2)	Floor area	50,000	24,000	15,000	11,000
Buildings insurance (W3)	Floor area	15,000	7,200	4,500	3,300
Equipment depreciation (W4)	Carrying amount of equipment	9,000	3,600	4,950	450
Equipment insurance (W5)	Carrying amount of equipment	6,000	2,400	3,300	300
Total overheads (a)		213,300	83,365	66,885	63,050
Re-apportion administration (W6)		–	44,135	18,915	(63,050)
Total overheads (b)		213,300	127,500	85,800	–

(c)   Overhead absorption rates:

Hair   £127,500 ÷ 8,500 = £15.00 per hour

Beauty   £85,800 ÷ 5,200 = £16.50 per hour

W1   Receptionist's salary

   Hair   £17,500 × 60% = £10,500

   Beauty   £17,500 × 40% = £7,000

W2   Rent and rates

	Square metres		£
Hair	240	240 ÷ 500 × £50,000	24,000
Beauty	150	150 ÷ 500 × £50,000	15,000
Administration	110	110 ÷ 500 × £50,000	11,000
Total floor area	500		50,000

W3   Buildings insurance

	Square metres		£
Hair	240	240 ÷ 500 × £15,000	7,200
Beauty	150	150 ÷ 500 × £15,000	4,500
Administration	110	110 ÷ 500 × £15,000	3,300
Total floor area	500		15,000

W4   Equipment depreciation

	Equipment £		£
Hair	18,000	18,000 ÷ 45,000 × £9,000	3,600
Beauty	24,750	24,750 ÷ 45,000 × £9,000	4,950
Administration	2,250	2,250 ÷ 45,000 × £9,000	450
Total carrying amount	45,000		9,000

W5   Equipment insurance

	Equipment £		£
Hair	18,000	18,000 ÷ 45,000 × £6,000	2,400
Beauty	24,750	24,750 ÷ 45,000 × £6,000	3,300
Administration	2,250	2,250 ÷ 45,000 × £6,000	300
Total carrying amount	45,000		6,000

W6   Re-apportion administration overheads

Hair   £63,050 × 70% = £44,135

Beauty   £63,050 × 30% = £18,915

CHAPTER 13: STANDARD COSTING AND VARIANCE ANALYSIS

1.   D

   (1,400 – 1,200) × £12 = £2,400 Fav

2.   A

   £15,200 – (1,400 × £12) = £1,600 Adv

3.   B

   1,100 × (£22.00 – £21.50) = £550 Fav

4.   C

   £22.00 × (1,000 – 1,100) = £2,200 Adv

5.   (a) and (d) are correct.

   (b) and (c) are incorrect.

6.   (c)

7. (a) Materials variance

(580 × £10.50) – (560 × £11.75) = £490 Adv

Possible causes could be:

- this is the overall variance, there will probably be some link between the price (£700 Adv) and usage (£210 Fav) variances, such as:

  – a better quality of material has been used, but at a higher price

(b) Materials price variance

560 × (£10.50 – £11.75) = £700 Adv

Possible causes could be:

- changing to a more expensive supplier

- not taking advantage of discounts available

- incorrect standard

- unexpected inflation

(c) Materials usage variance

£10.50 × (580 – 560) = £210 Fav

Possible causes could be:

- better quality of material

- more experienced staff, therefore generating less wastage

- incorrect standard

8.   (a)

	Original budget	Flexed budget	Actual	Variances
	£	£	£	£
Sales (W1)	96,000	108,000 *volume 12,000 Fav*	103,500	4,500 Adv *price 4,500 Adv*
Less costs				
Labour (W2)	28,000	31,500	37,440	5,940 Adv *rate 3,510 Fav* *efficiency 9,450 Adv*
Contribution	68,000	76,500	66,060	10,440 Adv
Overheads	30,000	30,000	30,000	–
Profit	38,000	46,500	36,060	10,440 Adv

W1   Sales

Original budget $80 \times £1,200 = £96,000$

Flexed budget $90 \times £1,200 = £108,000$

Actual $90 \times £1,150 = £103,500$

W2   Labour

Original budget $10 \times 80 \times £35 = £28,000$

Flexed budget $10 \times 90 \times £35 = £31,500$

Actual $13 \times 90 \times £32 = £37,440$

(b)   The actual sales price is lower than budget, which could be due to:

- wanting to secure more projects
- competition in the market place
- discounts for repeat business

The volume of sales is higher than the budget; causes could be:

- lower sales prices
- less competition
- seasonal increases

The labour rate is lower than allowed for, possibly due to:

- lower grade of labour used
- reductions in the level of wage rates

The labour efficiency is lower than expected, this could be due to:

- lower grade of labour used
- projects could be more complex than anticipated

CHAPTER 14: CAPITAL INVESTMENT APPRAISAL

1. C

Year	Net cash flow	Cumulative net cash flow
	£	£
0	(700,000)	(700,000)
1	(100,000)	(800,000)
2	600,000	(200,000)
3	850,000	650,000
4	250,000	900,000

Payback = 2 years + (200,000/850,000 × 365) = 2 years and 86 days

2. A

Year	Net cash flow	Discount factor	Discounted cash flow
	£	£	£
0	(700,000)	1.0	(700,000)
1	(100,000)	0.909	(90,900)
2	600,000	0.826	495,600
3	850,000	0.751	638,350
4	250,000	0.683	170,750
Net present value			513,800

3. (c)

4.   **Benefits** of the payback method include any one from the following:

- Payback is easy to calculate, cash inflows and outflows are added together cumulatively for each year, to identify when the initial cost of investment is repaid.

- Payback is easy to understand, by calculating the cumulative cash flows, it can be seen when an investment will be repaid.

- With payback, emphasis is placed on the earliest cash flows, which are probably more accurate than cash flows from a long time in the future.

Limitations of the payback method include any one from the following:

- Cash flow estimates may be inaccurate, which could mean that the wrong project is selected.

- Payback does not consider the cash flows after the payback period, which may have a major impact on a project.

- Payback does not take into account the time value of money, it assumes that a pound received now will be worth the same as a pound received in the future.

5.   **Financial** factors include any two from the following:

- initial capital requirements

- working capital requirements

- costs of borrowing

- taxation

- accuracy of cash flow and budget forecasts

Non-financial factors include any two from the following:

- expertise of employees required

- recruitment and training needs

- impact on the local economy and environment

- availability of material requirements

6.   (a)

Year	Net cash flow	Cumulative net cash flow
	£	£
0	(88,000)	(88,000)
1	23,000	(65,000)
2	65,000	–
3	72,000	72,000
4	87,000	159,000
5	12,000	171,000

Payback = 2 years

Net cash flow workings

Year 1   £76,000 – £38,000 – £15,000 = £23,000

Year 2   £160,000 – £80,000 – £15,000 = £65,000

Year 3   £174,000 – £87,000 – £15,000 = £72,000

Year 4   £204,000 – £102,000 – £15,000 = £87,000

Year 5   £54,000 – £27,000 – £15,000 = £12,000

(b)

Year	Net cash flow	Discount factor	Discounted cash flow
	£	£	£
0	(88,000)	1.0	(88,000)
1	23,000	0.909	20,907
2	65,000	0.826	53,690
3	72,000	0.751	54,072
4	87,000	0.683	59,421
5	12,000	0.621	7,452
Net present value			107,542

7.   **Assessment of the financial implications of the two projects:**

Initial investment – X is preferable:

- the amount for Y is double that of X
- the initial investment must be financed by a loan
- the interest rate on the loan is variable, therefore it could increase

Net present value – Y is preferable:

- the net present value of Y is much higher than X, meaning it will generate more cash
- a change in the interest rate would change the net present values of the projects
- a change in the return on capital employed would also change the net present values of the projects
- how reliable are the cash flow forecasts?

Payback period – Y is preferable:

- Y pays back in two years, whereas X takes three years
- however, the cash flows after the payback period are not taken into account
- how reliable are the cash flow forecasts?

Estimated life of the project – X is preferable:

- the project life of X is three years more than Y
- how reliable are the estimates?
- what happens at the end of the project, can the life be extended?

Assessment of the non-financial implications of the two projects:

Project X

- local residents are likely to object to the closure of a thriving community meeting place

- local jobs will not be created

- a new shop could cause disruption to local roads and parking

Project Y

- local jobs will be created in a deprived area

- sports facilities will become all-inclusive

- there are health benefits to encourage sports for all the local community

- there may be disruption to local roads and parking

Conclusion

Based on the financial factors, project X is less risky as the investment is lower, however, based on long-term cash flows and the assumption that the overall aim is to maximise the net present value, the choice should be project Y.

The non-financial factors would also indicate that the choice should be project Y.

However, Nottingsham Sports Ltd could also consider helping the community shop in project X to become more profitable by offering a range of sportswear in the existing shop.

Note: In a question of this nature, make sure you are able to back up your decision with valid points.